CALLED TO SERVE

With All Your Heart, Might, Mind, and Strength:
Missionary Preparation Series
ISBN 1-56236-000-0

Volume I: Prepare to Serve (ISBN 1-56236-001-9)
Volume II: Called to Serve (ISBN 1-56236-002-7)
Volume III: Continue to Serve (ISBN 1-56236-003-5)

Published by Aspen Books
893 South Orem Blvd., Orem, Utah, 84058

Cover design by Stewart Anstead, Aspen Design

Volume discounts available by calling Aspen Books toll-free
1-800-777-8226

WITH ALL YOUR HEART, MIGHT, MIND, & STRENGTH

Missionary Preparation Series-Vol. 2

CALLED TO SERVE

Marc Stephen Garrison

ASPEN
BOOKS

Orem, Utah

Dedication

This series of books is dedicated to Parley P. Pratt, whose missionary zeal inspired me, and to my parents who recognized the gospel message when two Elders knocked on our door. I love you Mom and Dad. I also dedicate this book to each missionary who at the end of a hard day's proselyting has gone on to knock on one more door, to make one more contact.

You are heroes.

When I began writing these books it was for my own children and Hokan and Johan, two young men whose testimonies blaze in the far reaches of Northern Sweden. After several months, I began to realize that I was really writing for anyone who, like myself, truly has desires to serve "With All Their Heart, Might, Mind and Strength."

Acknowledgments

Special thanks to Richard Oscarsson. You were not only a mission-ary president, you were a friend who taught by example. I thank both you and your wife from the bottom of my heart for serving so diligently in the Sweden, Stockholm Mission. Both you are your family taught me to love missionary work.

Special thanks also to Steve, Joe, Peggy and Nancy for their help and encouragement in completing this book.

Contents

Note For Parents

Taken individually each of the stories and chapters from these three volumes could be used as the basis for family home evenings. For example, starting with Book I—*Prepare to Serve*, Chapter 1, you might base a family home evening around the concept of "The Responsibilities and Blessings of Serving on a Mission." You could begin the lesson by singing a missionary song such as "Ye Elders of Israel", then have someone read the true story which the chapter begins with. After reading the story you could review and discuss the ideas that are described in that particular chapter. Depending on the age of your children, individual scriptures and reports could be assigned to be read from that chapter. The remaining twenty chapters could be used for the next twenty weeks, or mixed in with other activities or lessons depending on your family's needs.

Note for Missionary Preparation Teachers: Chapters can be combined and used for a 12-week missionary preparation course. Each prospective missionary should have read each of the designated Chapters prior to each meeting. Individual reports and assignments could be derived from each of the lessons. Group discussion and role play would be an integral part of using these chapters as learning tools.

Book I — *Prepare to Serve*

Week 1	Chapters 1 and 2
Week 2	Chapters 3 and 4
Week 3	Chapters 5 and 6
Week 4	Chapters 7 and 8
Week 5	Chapters 9 and 10

Book II — *Called to Serve*

Week 6	Chapters 1 and 2
Week 7	Chapter 3
Week 8	Chapter 4
Week 9	Chapters 5 and 6
Week 10	Chapters 7

Book III — *Continue to Serve*

Week 11	Chapters 1, 2 and 3
Week 12	Chapter 4, Review and Testimony meeting

Chapter 1

Missionary Conduct

If a man has a talent and cannot use it,
he has failed. If he has a talent and uses
only half of it, he has partly failed.
If he has a talent and learns somehow to
use the whole of it, he has gloriously succeeded,
and won a satisfaction and a triumph few men ever know.

Thomas Wolfe

Scriptures:
Alma 39:11, D & C 104:23, 2 Nephi 32:9, D & C 104:25,
1 Corinthians, Chapter 7

Elder Heath
Bolivia Mission

*As he stared out the window, his memories took him back in time
to the first week of his mission. The Missionary Training Center was a
great place to be, but everything was moving too fast. Bewildered and
confused, the young elder kept trying desperately to do his best not to
become discouraged, but despair and loneliness couldn't be defeated.*

Then one sunny afternoon as he stood alone gazing at the mountains shining in the brilliant sunlight, he felt his Father's love encompass his whole being. To be filled with such an immense feeling of love and understanding was the greatest gift he had ever felt.

"I want very much to share this love with the people of Bolivia. Please Father, guide me to those who are in need of our love."

He had come to this place when it was covered in darkness. All he could see of his new home then was a huge hole filled with innumerable lights. Now those same lights were beginning to reveal themselves outside the window where he sat gazing silently. A smile crept across his face as he watched the people passing by on the street below.

How great was his love for these people.

A valued memory echoed in his ears and played across his inward eye. "May God bless that tall, blond man who was kind to me when it was raining so hard, and I was desperately searching for something that would keep my little sister warm."

He remembered it was pouring down rain like he, a young, green missionary, had never experienced before in his life. There he was, out in the middle of it all, mud splashing everywhere, especially on his pants and overcoat.

"What are we doing out here," he grumbled to himself. "What's the meaning behind getting so cold and wet just to visit some members? If we are going to be out in this kind of weather freezing to death, we should at least be looking for someone to teach. I wonder if my trainer ever gets tired? I wish he would slow down so I could walk beside him, instead of by myself, five steps behind him."

Amidst his own troubled thoughts he noticed someone whose situation was far worse than his own.

4

"Oh, look at her! She isn't even wearing a coat."

The little girl, who passed him by quickly, wore only a dirty dress; no shoes or socks, no sweater or coat; just the dirty dress.

"She can't be very old. It isn't fair that someone so young should look so miserable and helpless."

The thoughts of the many suffering Bolivians somehow made him hurt inside.

"I wonder how much farther we have to go up? It seems like we are always walking uphill."

"Why don't you turn around and see if that little girl without a coat needs help?" an inner voice whispered.

"No, I can't stop," he thought. "My companion will leave me." Silently, he kept trudging up the hill without slowing down.

"Hey! Turn around and see if she needs some help!" the voice urged.

"I can't stop now. She's too far away, and anyway, there are lots of people that are as cold as she is."

"Are you just going to forget her, and catch up to your companion?"

With each step he took, the young missionary was bothered that he couldn't ignore the voice inside that was taunting him. Feeling as if he might burst if he took another step forward, he finally obeyed the unrelenting voice he felt and heard so strongly.

"Hey, Elder, will you wait a second? I have to do something."

As he turned to run down the hill towards the girl, who now was almost out of sight, he felt good.

"Excuse me, miss. Hi! My name is Elder Heath. When I passed you I couldn't help noticing that you didn't have a coat or anything to keep yourself warm. Please take this money and go buy something that will keep you warm."

Water dripped from her black hair onto her brown skin, then to the ground; she stood motionless for a moment, then took the money and ran down the hill without saying a word. The expression of joy and gratitude on her face told him all he needed to know of her feelings words couldn't express.

The wind and rain continued to make the day very cold and dreary as he turned to walk up the hill. He smiled at the mud as it jumped up onto his pant legs, not feeling the cold rain as it ran down his face, joining the tears that were flowing as freely as the rain.

"Well, only a few more hours and I'll be gone. I can't believe I will have to leave all of this behind."

The day was being chased away by the creeping shadows of dusk, those shadows that always seem to disguise the harsh reality that life in Bolivia holds for her inhabitants.

As he lingered over his memories, he knew that his hopes and prayers had been realized.

He couldn't see the people in the street very well now, only the lights. Soon, all would be out of sight; perhaps for a very long time. But he would remember and cherish the many he loved as he served the Lord in Bolivia.

•   •   •

"Wherefore, as ye are agents, ye are on the Lord's errand; and whatever ye do according to the will of the Lord is the Lord's business." (D & C 64:29.)

As missionaries of the Gospel of Jesus Christ, you are on the "Lord's errand." Can you sense what an awesome responsibility that is? You are being given stewardship over a portion of the Lord's vineyard, and you are charged with the responsibility of seeing that all nonmembers within your stewardship are given the opportunity of accepting or rejecting the Gospel of Jesus Christ. You hold salvation in your hands, and through you, the gates of eternal life are brought within reach to those who have been living in darkness. As a powerful, testimony-bearing messenger of the restored gospel, you become a savior to those whose lives you change. And it's all because the Lord loves you enough to allow you to become a partner with Him in His great work and glory: "to bring to pass the immortality and eternal life of man."(Moses 1:39.)

In Exodus 3:5, the Lord tells Moses to "put off thy shoes from off thy feet, for the place whereon thou standest is holy ground." When you're out there in the mission field, serving where a prophet of God has called you to serve, you are standing on holy ground. In much the same way as Moses was called out from the world and sent to deliver the children of Israel from bondage, you have been called and sent to take the liberating truths of the gospel to God's children throughout the world. The ground on which you're standing is, indeed, holy ground, sanctified by great men and prophets who have stood there before you. Do you approach it with an attitude of reverence? To be effective, you must put off the shoes of inappropriate behavior and worldly attitudes. Cast far away from you the shoes of improper language and selfish habits. Likewise, the shoes of impatience and intolerance for others have no place in the mission field.

In the MTC you will be taught the history and culture of your mission area. You have the advantage of being instructed by returned missionaries who can help you understand the people you are called to serve. They also understand the culture shock you as a missionary will experience. They can help you prepare for this shock and can help you avoid discouragement and homesickness.

Consider the following scriptures: D & C 90:11 and D & C 90:15.

In D & C 90 the Lord has declared that every man will be able to hear the gospel in his own tongue. You are privileged to be a part of this promise from the Lord to his children.

> *Our missionaries are going forth to different nations, and . . . the Standard of Truth has been erected; no unhallowed hand can stop the work from progressing; persecutions may rage, mobs may combine, armies may assemble, clumsy may defame, but the truth of God will go forth boldly, nobly, and independent, till it has penetrated every continent, visited every clime, swept every country, and sounded in every ear, till the purposes of God shall be accomplished, and the Great Jehovah shall say the work is done.* (Joseph Smith, *History of the Church,* 4:540.)

No matter how surprised you are when, with trembling hands, you open that letter from Salt Lake City and find out where you will spend your mission, you will soon begin to feel that mission to which you are called is exactly where you should be. As you study the culture, history, and religions of your mission area you will begin to feel an excitement about and appreciation for the people you are called to serve. Let this excitement grow. Even with the excellent preparation you will receive in the MTC, suddenly finding yourself in another culture is quite a shock. But, if you will determine to love the people before you reach your area, you will find adapting much easier.

You can learn about your mission area prior to your mission, by checking out books from your library or by watching travel films or documentaries about the area. In addition, you can almost always find at least one returned missionary in your stake or a neighboring stake who has served in your mission area. Ask to come visit with them and hear about their missions. A word of warning: be prepared to stay a long time and listen to a host of stories. You might also look up some recipes for ethnic food from your area and try cooking them for your family and friends.

Local Members and Church Leaders

Missionary work is really the responsibility of the local Church members who are to be deeply involved in finding, friendshipping, and fellowshipping. The trouble is many members are afraid to share the gospel or feel awkward or inexperienced in doing so. But you, as a trained specialist, can help them with this responsibility. Ideally, members should find and friendship investigators and fellowship them after they are baptized. Missionaries should teach members' investigators the basic principles of the gospel as contained in the proselyting discussions. Missionaries should answer investigators' questions in a clear, helpful manner (remember the importance of study). If members are to trust you enough to learn from you and let you teach their friends, you must show them by your humility, preparedness, and diligence.

I recall, as a zone leader in Sweden, getting a phone call one evening from two elders who were also serving in the same town. They asked if we could help them out, as one of the companions was sick and they had an appointment scheduled with a lady in the ward to teach some of her friends. Since my companion was sick also, I suggested that he find a member to stay with his companion and I would leave my companion with the members we lived with and the two of us could go out together. Since it was his area, I told him to work something out and give me a call back. I put my companion into bed, cleaned up the apartment and started doing some reports. The next thing I knew, it was 10:30 p.m. and I hadn't heard back from the elder.

The following day in church, I was approached by a new member of the church who appeared distraught. She related a story of how these Elders had set up an appointment with her several weeks before, and had encouraged her to invite all her friends and relatives to meet the missionaries and to see a film. They were going to have a little bit of an open meeting where the missionaries could answer any questions that her relatives or friends had, so that they could be introduced to the gospel. The Elders had set this up. She had invited friends and relatives, and spent several days preparing food. They came. In my mind I could see a picture of this new member of the church, strong, but not the strongest, with her friends over, waiting for the missionaries to come. The missionaries never did come, and they didn't call. Instead, this lady found out in church the next day from another member that a young girl in the branch had invited the missionaries over to see a movie and to spend the evening with her and her family. The missionaries had done that instead. They had not shown up to their commitment, but had instead gone and spent some time with this girl. The Elders were severely reprimanded but, still a great opportunity had been lost. I kept thinking of the lasting effect that their irresponsibility must have had on those friends of this new member.

The ability to work with the members in your area will be one of the greatest skills you can acquire as a missionary. Before I give you a list of things that will enhance your member-missionary work, let me give you a list of don'ts. You will likely encounter at least one area on your mission that is suffering precisely because earlier missionaries engaged in several of these "don'ts".

Don't solicit dinner invitations. No matter how the members beg and plead, accept invitations to eat only occasionally. And when you do, don't stay more than forty-five minutes to an hour. The members may plead for you to stay longer, but in the back of their minds they will wonder why you are not out teaching. In addition, they may think that feeding you fulfills their missionary obligation — WRONG.

To work successfully with the members in your mission area, remember the following:

- Don't become separated from your companion.

- Look alert; be direct; be well-groomed.

- Don't argue with members or your companion.

- Never criticize local leaders.

- Practice positive attitudes; eliminate the negative.

• Don't counsel members about personal problems. That is what branch presidents and bishops are for.

• Don't ever be alone with members of the opposite sex. It will set missionary work back ten years (even though nothing happens).

• Don't complain about the local religion, food, or customs.

• Never chastise members for their lack of missionary work.

• Don't speak a language they don't understand in members' presence.

• Never break mission rules. Some members might not even know if you do, but there are many returned missionaries who will, and will automatically lose respect for you.

Here are some things you can do to build up member work in your area:

• Thank the members for all of their missionary efforts.

• Compliment leaders and teachers for their fine leadership and instruction.

• Keep your clothes clean and your hair neatly trimmed.

• Show a sincere interest in the members and their own lives.

• Show a sincere love and respect for your companion.

• Ask members to share the gospel in ways that best suit their circumstances. For example, some families may be very shy about sharing the gospel. You might first ask them to friendship some of your investigators, thus helping them become comfortable talking about the gospel with non-members.

• Take priests and prospective missionaries with you to appointments or to proselyte.

When you go into different cultures, don't always talk about your culture. People are impressed with common courtesy. Quite often missionaries are invited out to dinner. We don't always realize the sacrifice that it may take for someone to invite a missionary over. Many families in foreign countries or even parts of the United States are on very limited fixed budgets. For them to invite some starving missionaries over, who are going to eat them out of house and home, is quite a sacrifice. One thing that I learned on my mission was that when you're invited over, always make it an experience that's fun. You don't go and live there. Go when you're invited, and bring a little gift. Even if you don't have a lot of money, you can pick some flowers in the summer. Even go and knock on someone's door and say, "Oh, I love your flowers. Do you mind if I pick a few? I'd like to take them to a friend." We would do things like that. It's that little touch that matters. Always remember that there will be Elders coming after you that are going to have to live up to your reputation. Then, after you've been invited over spend a stamp and send a note that simply says, "Thank you for inviting us over. We're excited to maybe meet some of your friends, and introduce the gospel to them, if we can help in any way." Turn every invitation into a missionary experience. It's not just a social one; it's a missionary one. You're not there to relax, but you are there to help challenge them and then build them up. One of the big ways to do this, I think, is through children, by being their friends and by being an example. If there are boys and girls in the family, first of all let them see you as being normal, then as someone who is deeply in love with missionary work, and who is really having fun. We also had a lot of opportunities in Sweden to extend common courtesies to women. It's so easy as a missionary, because you are always rushing around doing things which brings you into constant contact with others. When you rush into a store to grab yourself a loaf of bread and a carton of milk, be mindful of the lady behind. Don't run in the door ahead of her, but instead, stop and open the door for her. Try letting ladies get off buses first. Just the simple act of opening the doors for the ladies at church as they go into the chapel, helping them take off their coats, or helping them put their coats on at the end of church. It helps them feel a greater affinity with missionary work, makes them want to recommend you to their friends more, makes them want to be a greater part of the missionary effort.

When you are with the members, ask them if they have reservations or fears about sharing the gospel and then suggest ways to overcome those reservations. Try to always listen with an open mind to their words. You have to have an open mind to be able to resolve concerns.

A returned missionary I am acquainted with told me of one particular blind lady in a small town in North Carolina, a very beautiful woman with a great testimony. She had been blind for the past several years due to an illness. Her household was meticulously clean and neat. She would invite them over, and to be honest, she would serve them the worst food the missionaries had had in their lives. Food that your dog would turn down. Because of her handicap, when she'd make things, she might forget to put the sugar in lemonade, maybe not cook the meatballs thoroughly, or leave the milk out on the counter, so it would spoil. Then she would proceed to make the gravy out of sour milk. It was with great efforts that they'd even go and eat her meals. When they went the first time, one was just a new Elder and nobody had warned him. He sat down at the table and took a big helping of everything, and then took a big gulp of the lemonade. He couldn't stand it. It was straight lemon juice. He poured it into a plant near the table. (He went back a month later and saw the plant had died. She probably never noticed.) He still had an entire plate full of food to deal with. He ended up having to sneak it away. She couldn't see. The young green missionary learned a great lesson that day. You take small portions, then if you don't like it, you don't have to eat that much. If you take big portions, you are going to have to suffer. If you do like the food, after taking a small helping, you can take more. Common courtesy is to eat what you take. Nothing is more offensive to someone than to leave a plate full of food.

Also, in some European countries and parts of Asia, it is very rude to sit down and season your food before tasting it. They believe that they have prepared it the way that it should taste just right. If, after having tasted the food, you desire to season it, then that is all right. They realize that you may like it a little different, but to season before tasting is an insult to the cook.

This brings me to another aspect of missionary work: patience and empathy for the local members. Let me illustrate.

Have you ever seen a racehorse? Few animals seem more perfectly suited to gliding gracefully and quickly over a grassy meadow than a lithe and muscular quarter horse. Their speed and beauty are indicative of the task they have been bred to do.

And have you ever seen a plow horse? Tall and bulging with muscles, his very form speaks of power and strength.

Now which of the two animals do you think would win a quarter-mile sprint? The racehorse, right? And who would be able to pull that huge stump from the ground? The plow horse, right?

What does that have to do with missionary work? Well, full-time missionaries are a lot like racehorses. Racehorses eat, sleep, and breathe for one thing — to run. They are bred to do one task only — they are specialists. So are missionaries. They eat, sleep, and breathe missionary work. All they can think about is sharing the gospel. But a plow horse has to plow the fields, pull the wagon into town, give the kids a ride, and pull the neighbor's car from a ditch. He doesn't have the time to devote to racing only. Likewise members have to raise families, work, gain educations, serve in their community, and bake cookies for back-to-school night. Missionary work will be part of their lives (hopefully a part they take very seriously) — but it will always be only a part. You as a missionary need to respect their time and energies.

As a missionary you will ask the members to sacrifice. That's fine. But expect reasonable commitments of time and resources. And if members don't seem in as big as a hurry as you, realize that the people they convert will be a part of their lives for many years to come. They want their family and friends to have sound testimonies that are established on solid foundations which may take longer to build than the two months you are there. If you can develop a helpful, serving attitude with the members then they are much more likely to turn to you often. You can become the specialist with whom they consult.

One day I received a call from my mission president. He was going to open up a new area for missionary work. There were two Elders he wanted to put in a small town called Ornskoldvsvik. The president wanted me to go there as soon as possible to find an apartment for the Elders to live, and to generally get things prepared for the Elders to move there right away. There were several members there who had not been part of the church for quite some time, because there was no branch around. He asked me to go and meet them, tell them that they were loved, and that there would soon be missionaries there. I started calculating finances, and realized that if we took the bus to this small town it would use all of our money, and we wouldn't have any left for food. We figured that if we made the trip on our bicycles it would take us about eight hours, so we didn't know what to do. We called the branch president in the area and briefly related our situation to him. We asked him if there was possibly a member who, if we paid him for gas, could take us there sometime in the future. Without hesitation the Branch President said, "I'll take you there today." We asked him if he had to work. He said that didn't matter, and that he'd take us. He called his job, and said that he couldn't make it in. Then he picked us up, and we drove there that very day. We met the members. It was as if we were guided the entire day, and it was because of this fine Branch President. He took us to a real estate agent who helped us find an apartment that was nice, as well as the right price. We didn't have one obstruction the whole day. The branch president had helped us so much. As we returned that evening, we talked about how he had joined the church, about the temple, about his children, and about genealogy work. It was a very enjoyable day. When he dropped us off at our apartment, we took out money to pay him. As we did this he said to us, "You don't even realize what a blessing this day has been. If I had gone to work today, I would have done what I've done for years. You guys made me feel like a missionary today. I wouldn't take a dime." Letting other people help you like that is wonderful. It means being humble enough to let other people share some of the blessings. We didn't push ourselves onto the member, but we gave him the opportunity to help.

Let me mention a few other things that will help you keep member relations strong.

As mentioned before, you must never counsel members about their personal problems. Not only are you usurping their local leader's authority, but you are entangling yourself in personal matters that are none of your affair. Gossip can quickly spread when people are having personal difficulties and your name will be connected with it if you get involved where you ought not to. If members ask for advice about matters not related to missionary work, suggest that they talk with their local leaders and then voice your confidence in that leader's ability to help. You might also suggest some approved resource books for answers to doctrinal questions.

Missionaries and members should work together. But they report to different leaders: Missionaries report to the mission president; members report to ward or branch leaders. Full-time missionaries shouldn't command or instruct members in their duties. But they can and should *encourage* members and local leaders to do missionary work. Missionaries should meet with ward or branch mission leaders every week to coordinate their work with local member-missionary efforts.

Before you involve member families in missionary work, consult their local leaders and ask for their suggestions. They will be grateful that you respected their authority and can clue you in to members who are the most ready for missionary work. They can also inform you of members who might be under undue pressure or who may not be permitted to engage in missionary work. A simple check with local leaders can save you a great deal of time and possibly some embarrassment.

Regardless of how well you think you know the members in your area, you will find their local leaders can steer you in the right direction. They are entitled to inspiration for the members in their area and will best know whom you should approach and when. Also, you will find that in working with the local leaders you are much more likely to have their support and the use of their leadership skills to inspire members to share the gospel. Also, if the leaders are involved right from the start, then investigators and new members will feel much more at ease with them. As new converts grow in the gospel and the missionaries are slowly phased out of their fellowshipping, it is crucial that the new members have friends in the branch to whom they can turn for support.

Many members and leaders in developing areas of the Church are recent converts. Because they have had little time and experience in the Church, they may make some mistakes. Missionaries should support and strengthen local leaders and should never criticize them or attempt to advise them in areas outside of missionary work.

If you have a problem with local leaders, don't argue it out . . . take it to your mission leader. In Sweden, we had just found a beautiful, young family to be baptized. It was a single lady with several children. We'd taken them through the discussions. She had actually started living the Word of Wisdom before we'd even taught her the discussion on it. She had seen a television special on the Church, and heard how the members don't drink alcohol or smoke, so she quit everything the very night she'd heard it. It was a wonderful experience to teach this woman. As was customary, we called the branch president to arrange the baptism through him. Because we were about eighty miles away from the nearest branch, we asked for his permission, and also for him to meet her. For some reason he said that he wouldn't meet her and wouldn't let us baptize her. He said that he did not want another woman in his branch. While I was screaming at him on the phone, a thought occurred to me that I had heard in the mission home. Elder Richards had said that our mission president was our leader, and that branch presidents, bishops, and stake presidents are not our leaders. They have nothing to do with us. We do not get our baptisms approved by anyone other than just the correct priesthood authority. Elders had their district leaders interview the baptismal candidate, and district leaders have the zone leaders interview the baptismal candidate, then they are presented to the branch. Also, fellowshippers from the branch or ward should be used. We had used a lady in the branch as much as we could to fellowship our lady. It was a good experience. I hung up the telephone, and immediately called my mission president. I explained the situation to him, and magic happened. Within about twenty seconds I had a call from the Branch President. He apologized, and the baptism was arranged. This sister is a strong member of the Church today. She has since married and gone through the temple. Her son is ready to go on a mission, and the whole family is totally active.

As mentioned before, you can show support for local leaders by asking for their advice on how to conduct missionary work in your (and their) area. You can also strengthen them by thanking them privately and publicly for their leadership and service. Try as soon as possible to introduce them to any new investigators and keep them informed of the investigators' progress. Also, keep them up-to-date on all the proselyting within their geographical areas. Speak positively of them when in the presence of other members.

It is impossible to ignore the fact that there are local leaders, although you are not part of the leadership. I found it necessary, sometimes, to get to know these local leaders a little better than just on a Sunday-only basis. In one particular town we were the only missionaries for hundreds and hundreds of miles. We were also the only male members in this small town, besides the branch president and his counselor, who just about needed a wheelchair to get around. We decided that we would split up home teaching responsibilities of about thirty-seven women families. These two men had been home teaching all of these families. (And we complain sometimes because we have two or three families.) This was turned into one of the most positive experiences I've ever had. As we home taught with these men, we turned every single visit into a missionary experience by talking about their relatives or friends who might not be members of the church. We'd line up appointments to teach them. From those referrals we lined up more discussions in just a few hours than I had probably ever done in all of my tracting experience. Again, it was just working with some local leaders. They appreciated it, and it was a good experience. To this day, they are still doing that in the branch. The missionaries work with the part-member families, and help support them. It also helped us to realize how important it was for us to look for families with strong priesthood leaders who could help relieve some of the burden and help it to grow.

Mission Organization

Mission President. Your mission president is the presiding officer of your mission. He is responsible for every full-time missionary in your mission and looks out for the training and welfare of each missionary. Every four to six weeks, your mission president will conduct zone conferences where he will instruct and inspire you. There he will also have a personal interview with you. Aside from personal visits during zone conferences you will communicate with your president through written weekly reports.

Even though you may not have face-to-face contact with your mission president every week, you will find that he will become one of your closest friends and confidants. When you do have the opportunity to meet with him, be open and honest about how your mission is going. He is experienced and can offer level-headed advice and a perspective that you may not have. He can suggest ways to improve a tense companion relationship or how to work better with local leaders. You should retain this openness in your weekly reports.

As with any other Church leader, your mission president receives inspiration for the missionaries, members and direction of the work in his mission area. Give him your total loyalty and support. He will regularly ask the missionaries in the mission to focus their efforts on one particular method of proselyting or ask for their support in reaching various mission goals. The most successful missionaries are those who "go and do" what their mission president asks them to do. If he asks you and Elder Jones to tract forty hours per week, then tract forty hours per week. If he asks you to try street contacting, or member work, or anything else, then do it. And do it with the faith that your efforts will bring results. If your mission president asks you not to wear certain clothes or listen to certain types of music — then heed his advice. You will find that obedience to mission rules and guidelines will give you tremendous faith when calling on the powers of heaven for help in your work.

Other Missionaries. The organizational structure of the mission is as follows:

- Assistants — Two missionaries serve as personal assistants to the president and help him with logistical and spiritual planning.

- Office staff — Three to five missionaries serve in the mission office as mission secretary, recorder, financial secretary, and supply manager. The office staff proselyte in the evenings.

• Zone leaders — Two elders will supervise the missionary work within a specific geographical area of your mission. There are up to thirty missionaries in each zone.

• District leaders — Zones are divided into several smaller areas called districts. There are up to ten missionaries in a district. Each district is supervised by a district leader who will conduct weekly district meetings.

• Companions — Two missionaries work as a team and are responsible for the missionary work within a certain area of the mission.

During the course of your mission you may be called to any number of leadership positions in your area. Or you may never be called to any leadership position. It doesn't really matter. What does matter is that whatever call you are given that you go forward cheerfully and with desire to serve and succeed. It can be a frightening task to lead the missionaries in your district. And it can be even more frightening to be given the awesome task of training a missionary who just entered the field. As formidable as these responsibilities may seem, remember that the Lord does not give you assignments which you are not capable of carrying out.

It can be discouraging to many missionaries to have served perhaps their entire missions without ever receiving a leadership position in the mission. It should not be so, but it is. That is because often young, competitive and successful people are called to serve missions. And far too often they view success as "how high" they climb in the mission hierarchy. Missionaries often view a call to leadership in the mission as indicative of their level of spirituality. But ask any mission president and he will tell you that often his best missionaries never receive calls to leadership positions because they are too valuable as simply hard-working, humble missionaries doing what they do best — teaching the gospel.

Open up your scriptures and read and ponder the message of D & C 121:37.

We are instructed in D & C 121 that when we are called to a leadership position then we can only govern in meekness and without pride or vain attempts to control others.

Your Missionary Companion

As a missionary you will be assigned a junior or senior companion. You must always work two-by-two and should never be separated from each other. Please read the following scriptures: Mark 6:7, Luke 10:1 and D & C 42:6.

In ancient as well as modern times the Savior sent his missionaries out two-by-two.

Your companion will be a great support to you. If you and your companion work closely together, showing love and respect for one another and the gospel, then you can have a powerful effect on investigators. Please read: D & C 6:28.

In this scripture the Lord tells us that in the mouth of two or three witnesses every word would be established.

Your companion can also protect you from physical danger and temptation, and can stand as a witness in your defense when one or both of you is falsely accused. If you and your companion will stick together in body and spirit, then you can surmount almost any obstacle.

You should take seriously the charge to watch out for your companion's physical, emotional, and spiritual welfare.

Though it is not highly likely, there is a chance that you could be assigned a companion who has some serious problems with transgression and willfully violates mission rules. Despite your best efforts to set a good example and be a friend, you may be faced with the decision of whether or not to report your companion's transgression. This is a tough decision; let's hope you never have to make it. But if you do, remember this: Missionary work is serious business. You are not out on a student exchange program nor are you there on private matters or for a vacation. You are there as representative of the Lord. And while you may feel awkward in reporting serious transgressions, you have a weighty obligation to the Lord, to the other missionaries, to the members, and to your companion himself. It is your duty to watch out for and help your companion avoid transgression.

Many missionaries have been saved from great personal tragedy because of the faith, caring, and vigilance of their companions. But if you have one of the few missionary companions who won't listen to reason, you need to seek the advice of your mission president. You should know that if your companion is sent home for transgression he will likely be excommunicated or disfellowshipped. And if you willingly allowed him get in trouble and took no steps to prevent his straying, then you may also be excommunicated or disfellowshipped. Of course, I am not suggesting that you turn your companion in for sleeping late on preparation day. But you bear a tremendous responsibility to protect him and others from transgressing. The personal sins of a missionary can destroy the faith of members and investigators. Don't take lightly the trust of your mission president, the local members, your companion's family, or of the Lord. You must look out for your companion.

Even though you may never be involved in any missionary situation involving serious transgression, you should still take great care to ensure that even seemingly innocent indiscretions are avoided. Never become separated from your companion. Be cautious when talking to members of the opposite sex. Even situations that are totally harmless can take on unseemly appearances. And little things can become bigger things through gossip. Sure, you may be able to handle a little rock music, or a conversation with a member of the opposite sex while your companion is in another room. But think of other missionaries. They may not be able to handle it, and your bad example could lead them into situations they are not strong enough to deal with. So avoid even the little sins. They always lead to bigger sins.

In Sweden the winters are very intense, and quite often it will be dark twenty-four hours a day. The summers are equally as intense in the opposite direction. The summers last about two months, and the sun is up, and it is hot. In our mission we had a rule that we wore a suit, a tie, and a coat, and did not take the coat off. I always complained that in South America and South Africa they wore short sleeved shirts, and in Tonga they wore shorts and levis. But this was Sweden, and it was where we were called and we did what we were supposed to. I'll never forget one area I served in. We were often required to ride bicycles, sometimes for forty or fifty miles per day. This was just to cover the area, to meet people, and to follow through on contacts. That summer the temperatures reached nearly one hundred degrees fahrenheit. It used to be awfully enticing to take our coats off but my companion and I decided to leave them on. One day we were walking through a town, and decided to do some door contacting. At the third door we knocked on a young family answered. We introduced ourselves, and all this young family could say to us was, "Well, we're not real interested in the church, but why do you always have coats on? Don't you realize how hot it is? Those hills around here are steep, and we see you riding everywhere." We had an opportunity right there to talk about our missions. They invited us in, and gave us some cake and something to drink to cool us off. We had an opportunity right then and there to teach the first discussion. I can't claim this family was baptized, or much more than that they received the first five discussions and attended church several times. But gospel seeds were planted in the children and the parents. The only reason they were was because of those coats.

Companionship study and prayer will do much to strengthen the bonds of love and unity between you and your companion. You will find that study and prayer help you and your companion "tune in" spiritually with one another. When you teach, you will find that you can switch back and forth between each other with no noticeable transition. Also, as you study and ponder the scriptures you will also grow intellectually as each of you offers various insights.

The Lord has said, "If ye are not one, ye are not mine." Missionary companionships that are not unified inevitably flounder. It is much like two men trying to build a bridge from opposite sides of a ravine without any way to communicate. The chances are that neither of their efforts will ever meet or be completed. And one side of the bridge cannot stand for long without the support from the other side. Missionary work is the same way. If you and your companion try to build a solid proselyting effort without constant communication and an attitude of pulling together, then your efforts may never meet. On the other hand, if you and your companion can learn to communicate well, and plan and evaluate your proselyting program together then you will unlock the key to tremendous power and blessings.

As a missionary you will encounter opposition that you are not able to conquer alone. But with a companion by your side, together you can put up a united front that can overthrow that opposition. Each of you can offer unique perspectives, talents, and experience to whatever challenges you face, whether it be gaining the respect of the members, reversing anti-Mormon sentiment in the community, or simply finding people who will listen to your message.

You should always be loyal to your companion and constantly seek to build him or her up publicly and privately. Whatever differences you may have can be overlooked or resolved. Be a true brother or sister and friend to your companion. Please read 3 Nephi 11:29-30 and D & C 38:27.

Again, the Lord reiterates that if you will have His Spirit, then you must be one in purpose and heart with your companion. If not, then you are not the Lord's servants.

Like any other challenge on your mission, companionship friction can be overcome. If you find your companion relationship lacking unity and love, then try these steps:

One, you must realize that the little things don't matter. Little personality quirks may seem to drive you crazy right now. But they really don't matter. If you don't believe me, then kneel down and talk to your Father in Heaven about them. Decide that you won't take notice of your companion's trivial idiosyncrasies. And hope that he, like you, decides the same. (Yes, you have them, and like your companion, you may not be aware of them.)

Two, earnestly pray for your companion every day. You will find as you talk with the Lord about him, then He will share His love for, and understanding of your companion with you. And you will soon begin to love your companion much more.

Three, look for the good in your companion every day. Take a few weeks and see if you can't list just one different quality that you like about your companion every day. Keep your mind focused on the positive. When those negative thoughts gnaw at you, remember their source is not the Lord.

Four, take a week and consider your companion as if he were the Savior. Every time you are about to say or do something unkind, ask yourself if you would do this to the Savior. It was Jesus of Nazareth who told us that how we treat the "very least" among us is how we would treat Him. Learn this principle as a missionary and you will have acquired the key to one of life's greatest freedoms — control of our own feelings and emotions.

Even though you can learn to overcome harsh feelings for your companion, there are still times when you will have to suggest he change his behavior. Sometimes missionaries act in a way that is not dignified or that makes you feel unappreciated. Sometimes they rationalize the breaking of "small" mission rules. If so, you will have to correct their behavior. The first rule here is to be prayerful. As you discuss the problem with your Father in Heaven, He will influence you in what you should say and when you should say it. And when you do correct your companion's words or actions, do so kindly. There is no excuse for adding insult or hostility — even if you must speak sharply to reprove your companion. If you can offer constructive criticism with a spirit of love, then your companion will always know (even if it takes a while for him to come to that realization) that you have his best welfare at heart.

Always foster love and respect for your companion. It can help you develop love and respect for yourself and the members and non-members in your area. It can also influence investigators.

One way to nurture love and respect is to regularly do kind acts of service for your companion. You can get every morning off to the right start by making your companion's bed. You can shine his shoes, or iron his shirt. By doing chores that are obviously his responsibility, you can create a spirit of service that makes your work more enjoyable. A junior companion's perspective changes when he becomes a senior companion. Suddenly he wishes he had been the kind of companion he longs for now. For example: It was Elder Rigby's first preparation day as a senior companion. Before he even wrote to his parents, he wrote a letter to Elder Conley, his former senior companion. "I never realized how tough it was being a senior companion," he wrote. "I hope you will forgive me for the times when I didn't support you." The next week he received a letter from Elder Conley. "It's O.K.," responded Elder Conley, "I wrote a similar letter to my former senior companion when I was made a senior. He had also once written the same kind of letter."

You can make it through your mission without ever writing such a letter. How? Put yourself in your senior companion's shoes right now. Overcome any ego hangups about being a junior companion and support your senior companion as if he were your older brother (he really is, you know). Show respect for his leadership. Decide now that you will excel as a follower. Certainly your input is just as important as his. But when the time comes that a choice has to made one way or the other, support his decision. When it comes to choosing Plan A or Plan B, you will learn that making the right choice really depends most on making the choice right. It is your companionship unity and persistence that will make a plan successful or not. And it is learning to follow that teaches you how to lead.

Be sure to always speak with respect to your companion, showing deference to his or her calling as a servant of the Lord. Call your companion by his appropriate title, never just "Elder," or "Sister'" or "Smith."

You and your companion must keep the lines of communication constantly open. This openness can prevent negative feelings from growing and can keep misunderstandings to a minimum. Each week (more often if needed) you and your companion will conduct a "companion inventory," a meeting wherein your discuss your companion relationship. Some mission-aries look at companion inventory as the time to air their gripes. But really it is a time to discuss aspects of your companionship and proselyting efforts that need improvement. Therefore, when you meet in companion inventory make it a time to evaluate past successes and use that knowledge and experience to plan greater successes for the future. Attack problems not people. Overlook the trivial. Make this meeting fun and solution-oriented.

I only had my first companion for about four weeks, then he returned home. When I arrived, it was the dead of winter; and his mission was ending. During the four weeks that we spent together I never heard one mention of home. I never heard one mention of anything related to home. He had a little chest he would pack things in quietly. He never said a thing, and he worked his tail off. It was as if the last four weeks he had were kind of like the last gasp of a dying man. A light bulb before it burns out gets real bright, and that is just what Elder Bateman did. He put everything he could into the last four weeks. His goal was to make me the best Elder there was. I realized later that he had developed a severe ulcer on his mission, but he never told anyone about it. He never complained. He always ate baby food. I used to make fun of him. Why was he eating baby food? That was really all his stomach could handle without causing him to throw up. The last four weeks we worked, we baptized, we saw great success and we never stopped. We were out the second it was time to go. We were back the second it was time to be back at night. We went to bed on time. I learned from him to love. He wasn't the most outgoing Elder that there was, or the most talented, but I've never seen anyone who loved people more than he did. The lesson I learned right from the start was that missionary work wasn't putting on a big front, it wasn't always looking impressive, it's hard work, but it's fun work and it's motivated by the pure love of Christ and our brothers.

Challenge

Review the section titled "Communication," in your *Missionary Handbook*, pp. 25-27. If you have had or are having a personality conflict right now with someone, practice the tools you are going to need on a mission by purposely seeking to restore that friendship or alleviate the problem.

If you are on your mission and do have a problem with your companion, try this. Sit down with your companion and read and discuss the sixth verse in D & C Section 4. There the Lord points out the qualities of a successful missionary companionship. "Remember faith, virtue, knowledge, temperance, patience, brotherly kindness, godliness, charity, humility, diligence." With the spirit of the Lord, your missionary companionship can have these qualities.

Chapter 2

Missionary Excellence

The best portion of a good man's life
— his little nameless, unremembered
acts of kindness and of love.

William Wordsworth

Scriptures:
D & C 75: 13-22, Alma 48: 12, D & C Section 89, D & C 107: 18,19

Sister Peggy
France, Mission

 I didn't want to go on a mission. I mean I really did not want to go on a mission. From the time I was a little girl I always had this idea that the only Sisters who went on missions were old spinsters who could not get married. As I got near 21 years of age, this girl at work started talking with me about a mission. It started me thinking, so I decided to pray about it. But you know how it is when you pray about something that you don't want to do. The girl at work wasn't the first, though, to bring up the idea of a mission. When I shared my patriarchal blessing with my sister, she said, "Peggy, look at this. It looks like you're going to go on a mission." I was horrified; that just wasn't possible. I ignored that memory and part of my patriarchal blessing until the girl at work started bringing up the idea of my going on a mission.

Pretty soon my bishop called me in and started talking to me about a mission. He said I really should go. For the next couple of months I could almost think of nothing else. The spirit was gnawing at me all day long. I even had trouble eating. All that I could think about was not going on a mission. Finally I told my bishop I would go. I have never been so scared of anything in my life. A few days later I called him back and told him to cancel the reservation. A few months after that I called him up and told him to get the papers ready. We hear a lot about free agency. I didn't want to go. But concerning my going on a mission it didn't seem like I had any choice. My mind said no, but the spirit kept winning the tug of war. So the bishop filled out my papers "in ink"

When I called up the doctor and dentist to arrange for my pre-mission check-ups I could hardly talk. All that I wanted to do was cry. One of the reasons why I was so scared still once I had made the decision is that I hate to speak in church. I hate role play and act out situations. I also knew that missionaries had to speak in church (and not just on their missions, they had to give homecomings and farewells) and role play in the MTC.

My papers were finally sent in on April 9th, my mission call came on April 29th by express mail. When I read where my mission was to be, I immediately went into shock. My call said that I had to report to the MTC in two weeks by May 15th (I didn't have a chance to back out). My bishop was frantic. With fast and testimony meeting the next week and Mother's Day the Sunday after that, he didn't know how he was going to fit in a farewell. I volunteered to go without. He chose instead to cancel the Mother's Day program.

If I were to sum up the MTC in one sentence it would be, "I enjoyed it a lot." On my first day, one of my greatest fears was realized when I had to participate in a group role play in front of a very large room full of new missionaries. I died as I participated in a demonstration in front of everyone about finding out the real concern. But that experience and hundreds of others helped me to grow. In the MTC I made a lot of friends with the other Sisters, and really felt that it was the perfect transition for me into full-time missionary life.

After a grueling "by myself" flight from SLC to Europe I finally got there three days later (I left on Wednesday morning and got there Saturday afternoon in the same dress). When I finally was picked up at the airport to meet my mission president, I died. I had tried so hard not to spill anything on my dress, but on the final flight I had spilled orange juice and I think the rest of my breakfast on my dress. I tried my best to clean it off, but I couldn't get rid of a big spot. Inspired, I took off my name tag and pinned it over the spot. I must have looked a sight when I came off the plane. But, all worries fell away when my mission president's wife encircled me with her arms and welcomed me to my mission.

One thing that my stake president told me before my mission was that I would probably have my greatest challenge with getting along with companions. I really wondered about that. I had always gotten along with people. But looking back now, I guess I had never lived in a fishbowl with someone before. I am really grateful for his advice. For any companionship to work, marriage, missionary, leadership, etc, there has to be patience, understanding, forgiveness and a double dose of giving. You have to be willing to let the other person have their way and you have to let the little problems ride. If you aren't willing to compromise, then you're going to spend all day arguing and get nothing accomplished.

I think my Stake President has been inspired in his prophetic words by my companion Sister J. When the zone leaders dropped me off at my new companion's boarding house, I was a little sick because of the transfer I had. I had really grown to love my companion, our investigators, the ward members and felt really at home in my old area. I had been there for six months so I guess a move had to come sometime.

So, here it was. When the Zone leaders left us alone, I looked around our one room flat. It had two small beds, a kitchen, a bath, a great view of the ocean and tons of cockroaches. It also had Sister J. She instantly took charge. In fact thinking back now, she never stopped talking for the next two months. I had never before lived with a someone who could talk like she did. It wouldn't have been so bad if she had had anything to say. But she seemed as if she had gotten mixed up over the proverb about "Silence is Golden". There were a few other things that really got on my nerves about her. (More so than any other Sisters I had worked with.)

So here I was. Stuck with a companion that drove me bananas. I felt compelled to seek an answer in prayer. As I prayed, asking Heavenly Father to help me overcome these negative feelings, I felt compelled to work hard. And that we began to do. As we immersed ourselves in work, we soon found ourselves coming home at night and literally dropping into bed dead tired from our missionary activities. It seemed like the harder that we worked, the happier we became and the more insignificant Sister J's little quirks became.

I even found myself starting to really like her. I look back now and realize that companionship could have gone two ways. I could have picked at her from the start about all the things that she did that bothered me. I could have started at the top of my list each day and "helped her improve" up to what my standard of what a missionary should be. If I had torn into her, I have no doubt that the result would have been a companionship that wouldn't have had any success. Even more tragic than that, perhaps she would have gone home, if I had encouraged her to leave, rather than discouraged her from doing so in her time of doubt. Instead, we worked hard together, and I ignored the little problems. I also realized that the things that bothered me about Sister J were a reflection of my own weaknesses. Her constant talking bugged me simply because I was a bit on the quiet side. Maybe if I had been more talkative, she wouldn't have talked so much. With Heavenly Father blessing me with this insight, and blessing both of us with the desire to really work hard, I ended up having some of my most spiritual experiences that I had on my mission with her.

One day we were driving from the area where Sister J and her previous companion had worked to our area. Before I knew what was happening, Sister J had flipped a "U" in the road, and we were headed back to the area. She took me to a place I didn't even know existed. She and her previous companion had tracked out a man who told them to come back, but with events that transpired after, they had not been able to return. She couldn't even remember his name. But never doubting her inspiration we walked up to his home. He was there, and welcomed us in. We were able to share the first discussion right then, still a little unsure of our purpose for coming back. He had a visitor staying with him who turned out to be his sister-in-law. She also sat in on the discussion. As the discussion progressed we found out that she had already been exposed to the Book of Mormon. In fact, she actually had one. Some missionaries had boarded with one of her relatives and had given her one. Only she had never taken the time to read it. As we presented the discussion, her interest was sparked, and she said she would have to find her copy of the Book of Mormon and read it. Then she told us something that clued Sister J and myself in on why we had to stop that very afternoon: She was leaving to return to her home 600-800 miles away the very next morning. As she said that, the Spirit bore witness to Sister J and myself individually that she was the reason we were there.

I lost track of her, and have no idea if she was ever baptized. One thing I do know is that Sister J and I were the happiest missionaries in the world as we drove from that man's home. The Spirit had prompted, and we had obeyed, not knowing at the time why, but then receiving the confirmation later. It was such a beautiful experience to be an instrument in planting the seeds of the Gospel. We didn't get to reap the reward of seeing that woman baptized, but it didn't matter to Sister J and myself, because we knew in our hearts that we had done exactly what Heavenly Father wanted us to do.

Sister J and I had many other wonderful experiences as we served the Lord together as companions. I am so grateful that Heavenly

Father helped me keep a perspective on the companionship and exactly what my real purpose for being there was. What a tragedy it would have been if I had dwelt on the negative, and let that eliminate the beautiful experiences we enjoyed together.

I will be eternally grateful that a loving Heavenly Father prompted me to know how to make a companionship work. I continued to use what I had learned about companionships and getting along with people the rest of my mission. In fact, I still use it today. I am so thankful that Heavenly Father had such a great amount of patience with me as I struggled to accept the call to serve, that the Spirit kept gnawing away until I finally gave in. My mission has definitely been the highlight of my life, and I would not have wanted to miss such a tremendous experience.

•   •   •

In the preface of the Doctrine and Covenants there is written what the Lord made known to the Prophet Joseph Smith that we are expected as a people to convey the message of the restoration to the masses of the world so . . . . "that every man might speak in the name of God the Lord, even the Savior of the world . . . . That the fullness of my gospel might be proclaimed by the weak and the simple unto the ends of the world and before kings and rulers."

To fulfill that challenge there can be no apathy within the ranks of missionary work. The enthusiasm and spirit of missionary work must be alive and active in the heart of every missionary. For this is the spirit of the Church.

As a missionary you will fill several important roles: teacher, ambassador for Christ, friend. As stated in your mission call you will be expected to maintain the highest standards of conduct and appearance by keeping the commandments, living mission rules, and following the counsel of your mission president.

Called to Serve

Please read Corinthians 9:14, D&C 65:29, 1 Timothy 4:12-16, and 3 Nephi 27:27.

The Lord has instructed his followers to live the very highest standards, indeed He has asked them to be like Him.

Excerpts from a Mission Call:

You have been recommended as one worthy to represent the Lord as a minister of the restored gospel. You will be an official representative of the Church. As such, you will be expected to maintain highest standards of conduct and appearance by keeping the commandments, living mission rules, and following the counsel of your mission president.

You will also be expected to devote all your time and attention to serving the lord, leaving behind all other personal affairs. As you do these things, the Lord will bless you and you will become an effective advocate and messenger of the Truth. We place in you our confidence and pray that the Lord will help you meet your responsibilities.

The Lord will reward the goodness of your life. Greater blessings and more happiness than you have yet experienced await you as you humbly and prayerfully serve the Lord in this labor of love among His children.

President Harold B. Lee has said this about achieving the highest standards:

You cannot lift another soul until you are standing on higher ground than he is. You must be sure, if you would rescue the man, that you yourself are setting the example of what you should have him be. You cannot light a fire in another soul unless it is burning in your own soul." (Harold B. Lee, *Ensign*, July 1973, p. 123.)

Guarding Your Thoughts

Because you are the Lord's agents, your conduct often influences the attitudes and feelings of both nonmembers and members. Your thoughts, words, and actions should always be in harmony with the spirit of the message you bear. Clean and uplifting thoughts are essential to missionary work. The Lord will work only through clean vessels. Wholesome thoughts lead to wholesome words and actions.

Please read the following scriptures: Proverbs 23:7, Matthew 5:27-28 and D & C 121:45-46.

The Lord has told us that we must think virtuous thoughts continually for as we think in our hearts so are we.

Idleness is the devil's workshop and the idle mind is open to all types of vulgar, discouraging, and distracting thoughts. Learn to discipline your thoughts and you literally set yourself free. A missionary in control of his thoughts is in control of himself and will be less susceptible to the negative influences of others. You can discipline your thoughts through memorizing one scripture or inspirational thought each day. When confronted with carnal or suggestive sights, immediately turn away. You can hum or quietly sing to yourself (although in some cultures this is consider poor behavior).

When you do listen to music listen to uplifting, wholesome music. And you can do as the Lord directs and pray constantly that you might not enter into temptation.

Guarding Your Words

The Church is often judged by the conduct of its missionaries. Your positive actions will bring positive results and your negative actions will bring negative results. Therefore, avoid the following:

• Do not become involved in contention or disputations over points of doctrine with members or people from other faiths.

• Do not become involved in public or private debates with members of other churches.

• Do not criticize other religions.

• Do not gossip or become engaged in vulgar conversations.

• Do not speak negatively of the culture or way of life in your mission area.

As a lifelong rule, consider the following scriptures: Ephesians 4:29 and D & C 108:7.

As these scriptures suggest, do all that you can to uplift and strengthen your brothers and sisters.

Few actions are a greater waste of time than arguing points of doctrine. On your mission you will constantly meet those who await to engage in a "discussion" about various points of doctrine. Whether you are contending with the minister of the local church, the Gospel Doctrine class instructor, or your companion, it is still contention. Sure, you will meet people who say things that will anger you. And yes, you will feel the desire to deflate their arguments. Certainly you can prove to them that their beliefs are false and ours are true. Right? Wrong.

You will constantly encounter others who want to convince you of the error of your ways. Don't waste your time bashing scriptures with them. When the spirit of contention enters a room, the Holy Spirit leaves. Simply bear testimony to them. If they wish to continue in an argumentative manner, then quickly leave. You have borne testimony of the truth. That is the purpose of your calling.

You will find individuals or groups who attack our church. Don't imitate their antics. Others may attack us but they CANNOT stop the work. It will go forward. Others may belittle us, but we must not belittle them. Never deride the beliefs of others. It indicates to those listening that you do not have confidence in your own beliefs. And it leaves an impression of you that is negative. Leave other religions alone. You have plenty of other assignments to carry out.

Guarding Your Actions

Your good example can open doors. Conversely, your bad example can slam them shut. Alma's missionary son, Corianton set a bad example which caused the Zoramites to disregard Alma's teachings. Read Alma's words to his son. Alma 39:11-13.

If you offend non-members of the Church, then they may excuse themselves from ever listening to the gospel message. If your conduct is not in keeping with your calling as a representative of Christ, then non-members will know that your message and your calling are not important to you. And if the gospel is not important to you, then why should they listen?

How you dress, speak, study and eat will affect your ability to communicate your message. As a result, the Church has developed specific guidelines for missionary conduct.

Guidelines for Conduct

Missionaries should dress cleanly, neatly, and modestly. A simple, yet comely appearance will give a quiet dignity to the overall impression you make. Your mission president will give you more specific guidelines, but in general the Missionary Handbook suggests that you:

- Dress conservatively. Elders should wear dark suits, white shirts and conservative ties. Lady missionaries should wear conservative colors, with skirts and dresses reaching to the knee or below.

• Have regular haircuts. Elders are expected to keep their hair above the neck, collar, and ears. Moustaches or beards, and long sideburns are prohibited.

In addition, polish your shoes, iron your clothes and keep them laundered or dry cleaned.

Use your precious time wisely. There will be variations from mission to mission yet your daily mission schedule might look like this:

A.M.	**P.M.**
6:30 .... Arise	1:00 .... Proselyte
7:00 .... Study class	5:00 .... Dinner
with companion	6:00 .... Proselyte
8:00 .... Breakfast	9:30 .... End proselyting, plan
9:30 .... Proselyte	next day's activities
12:00 ...... Lunch	10:30 .... Retire

Missionary couples may have schedules that vary according to their responsibilities.

All missionaries, regardless of their duties, will have far greater control of their lives if they can learn to plan effectively.

Planning should never control your life. But you will find as a missionary, as in other aspects of life, that planning will put you clearly in control of your day. You will have a clearly defined schedule that you will be expected to follow as a missionary. Though it will likely vary to some extent from the one listed above, you will be greatly blessed if you can follow the outline of the schedule which your mission president requests you to adhere to. It is especially important that you arise and retire on time so that you can be rested and have the energy and vigor to conduct your work. You should always make the time for personal and companion study of the scriptures, discussions (and possibly the language). You should also leave yourself the proper amount of time to cook and eat a nutritious meal.

What are your goals today? How will you achieve them? If you are an average person, then you might have been able to answer those questions only in vague, general terms. That is because most people refuse to set daily goals. Goal setting is a major part of success. But is only an effective tool for success if it is used properly. Anyone can set a goal. But only those who can use them properly achieve them.

Set realistic goals. Push yourself, but don't try to achieve the impossible. Those who set unrealistic goals are seldom successful — then goals take on a negative connotation for them. You can set achievable goals by drawing on past experience. Suppose your goal is to learn one new concept from the discussion on the plan of salvation. If your past attempts at learning one concept have taken one hour, don't set a goal to learn the concept in 20 minutes. Decide to learn the new concept in 55 minutes. You will still have to stretch, but you can realistically succeed.

Learn to plan. Planning prevents you from wasting your time because it gives form to your ideas and makes you think specifically. It will also help you keep track of your appointments.

Learn to think specifically. You and Elder Roberts have set a goal to find one person to teach today. This is a good goal; for one thing, it is attainable. But how will you achieve it? By thinking specifically. Let's walk through the process together.

First, what kind of person do you want to teach? Both of you decide that you want to contact a father.

When do you want to contact him? It will have to be this morning or this afternoon because you have appointments tonight.

Where will be the most likely place to find him? You decide the best place is downtown in the business district during the lunch hours.

Judging from past experience, how many men will you have to approach? You know from past attempts at street contacting that you will probably have to approach between twenty to twenty-five people before someone will express an interest to hear more about your message.

Should we work on the north side of the street or the south side? Who cares? We don't want to get that specific or we will get bogged down and planning will control us instead putting us in control.

All right, are there any other factors you need to consider? Yes, whoever we contact will likely have a limited amount of time so we may only be able to talk for five to ten minutes.

Given that time limit, what would be an appropriate topic to spark sincere interest? Modern day prophets have always sparked interest as has the Book of Mormon and the Plan of Salvation.

So which would be best? We will have to leave that open since the Spirit may inspire us differently for each individual we contact. However, we want to concentrate mostly on one topic so we will practice asking questions about the plan of salvation that cannot be answered with a yes or a no. Those who have no interest will simply brush us off, but an open-ended question will cause those who are receptive to ponder what we ask them. And we know that pondering brings the Spirit. And it is the Spirit that motivates people to learn about the gospel.

All right, now what have both of you specifically decided to do? Again, let's walk through it.

You and Elder Roberts have decided to find one father downtown during the hours from 11:30 to 1:30. You will ask each man you contact an open-ended question about the plan of salvation (although you are prepared to ask questions about modern prophets or ancient scripture). You have outlined a "mini-discussion" that you can teach in ten minutes since you know the men you contact will be pressed for time. You are prepared to approach at least twenty-five different men since you know that it may require that many attempts to find someone who is receptive. And finally, you decide that you will get his address and telephone number, *and an appointment* so that you can continue to teach him and his family the gospel.

There, you have done it. You not only set a goal, but you mapped out a way to achieve it. And it only took ten minutes to make all of those decisions. And since you and Elder Roberts have reached ninety percent of you goals in this manner, you feel confident of success.

The Church has said that for missionaries listening to appropriate music is an acceptable activity if it does not interfere with missionary responsibilities. The Church has generally urged that missionaries listen to LDS hymns and other sacred music. In some missions classical and other types of music are permitted. Your mission president will most likely have established some set mission guidelines for you to follow once you are in the field.

Music is communication. The melody and lyrics are always telling you something. Music can relax or agitate you. It can turn your mind towards your work or it can lull you towards distracting or unclean thoughts and actions. Although most types of music can be uplifting, your mission president will decide which types of music are appropriate for you to listen to. There is not much to say about your mission president's guidelines other than to follow them.

You have kept your mission president's guidelines regarding music. Now when can you listen to it? That may also depend on your mission president. Some say only on preparation day. Others say you may listen to it during meals or during periods of meditation. But I would suggest that even if you are permitted to listen to music any time you are in your apartment that you not listen while you are studying. While music will relax and uplift you, even the best music will also distract you from your studies. Some music is more distracting than other types, but all of it will detract from your study time. Listen before or after you study, but not during. If you will make this sacrifice, you will find your mind and spirit greatly rewarded.

Preparation Day

Preparation day, as the name suggests, is a day for you to prepare for the rest of the week. This is a day to take care of personal and temporal matters, such as letters home, laundry and shopping. It is also a day to relax and have some fun.

As with any other day of the week, you should carefully plan your preparation day. This will keep you from wasting time and allow you more time to do what you enjoy. Missionaries work hard and they should also play hard. As previously mentioned, you will want to engage in activities that don't distract you from the spirit of your work. However, after the shopping and letters are completed, you should still have time to immerse yourself in the culture and history of your area. Many missionaries can get an enviable education in culture, history, and even science, as they visit museums, art galleries, historical sites, etc. After you have seen to temporal affairs, be sure to have fun — and learn something too.

Preparation day should begin with study and prayer like any other day. This will help set the tone for the day and help you obtain the Spirit when you begin proselyting at 5 p.m.

Activities previously mentioned such as visiting museums should bring some side benefits besides entertainment and education. A trip to the local museum or exhibit will teach you more about the local culture and history, thereby making you more sensitive to the beliefs of the people you serve. In addition, if you can talk about items of local importance with non-members, then they will see you have made an effort to become familiar with their way of life and will therefore trust you more.

Local Laws, Customs and Traditions

Whether you are called to a foreign mission or to your own country, you are, in some ways, an outsider in your mission area. As such, you should respect the customs and traditions. Be discreet in what you say publicly and privately concerning local peoples, institutions, and conditions.

Missionaries were actually expelled from one Middle Eastern country because one missionary wrote negative comments about the country in a letter to a friend.

Suppose someone from another culture was visiting your house and made disparaging comments about your community and your culture. Would you have any desire to listen to him? Other people have similar feelings about their own culture. Even if they put it down, they would still be offended if you ridiculed their nation's practices and beliefs.

Sundays and Holidays

You should attend the appropriate Sunday meetings and in all other ways keep the Sabbath holy. Proselyting on Sunday is not only permitted, it is recommended.

In one part of my mission I was in a town that was quite isolated from another branch, about thirty or forty miles away — two and one half hours by bicycle. My companion and I figured out that the bus fare would be the equivalent of our week's worth of groceries, if we took the bus to church. So we decided to ride bikes to church. The Elders hadn't done that before. We steeled ourselves for the long trip. We needed to be at church by 9:30 a.m., and so we started riding about 6:00 a.m. We arrived about 8:45 a.m. We did that for about six months. It turned out to be one of the most glorious experiences I had. After a while we figured those early morning rises were getting a little bit too hectic, so we decided to work our area the Saturday night, then ride bikes to the town where this branch was located. While riding in the moonlight along the coast of Sweden, looking across the channel at the coast of Denmark, we had some great talks. We had some fun times on this lonely little two-lane road, windmills on each side, beaches, and beautiful trees and cliffs. Sometimes now when I get hassled and worried, I think back on that simple time. I think about the spare trash bag we'd carry in our back pockets in case it rained. When it did, we'd poke holes in the bags to stick our heads and arms through. We'd then keep on pedalling until we arrived at the other Elders apartment, where we'd sleep on the floor with a blanket. The next day we'd go to church. We would spend the rest of the day working with the other Elders in their town, then return to ours by Sunday night. When the local members heard what we were doing they seemed to take a little different look at missionary work. They started thinking more about the Elders way out and the Elders in town.

They tried to do a little more for us. They started thinking about the sacrifices made by the missionaries. I didn't look at it as a sacrifice though; I looked at it as sheer fun! There was a particular hill on the ride that I couldn't even come close to making it half way up. After about three months of making the trip, we could make it the entire way without even getting out of breath. Those were good times.

But I can still hear you gasping. Proselyte on Sunday?

You have been told your whole life not to work on Sunday. And now, as a missionary, you suddenly find yourself required to proselyte on Sundays. But you will find that the Lord set Sunday apart to be a day to rest from your labors in the world. But since you are laboring in the Lord's vineyard, proselyting is a fitting way to honor your Father in Heaven. And Sunday is an excellent time to proselyte. Families will be at home or in the park together. Some may have just come from religious services and thoughts of God may still be fresh in their minds. Most people will not be working on Sunday and will have time to listen to your message.

Like Sundays, holidays can be an excellent time for proselyting. Not only will families be at home together, but most holidays are either religious or patriotic in origin. The theme of each holiday can be incorporated into your proselyting efforts. During the Christmas or Easter seasons street displays about Christ's visit to the America's can generate great interest in the gospel.

Sacrifice Brings Blessings

Sometimes missionary success comes as a result of extreme sacrifices of efforts on the behalf of the missionary. The following story from Gunvor Wirtala shows just how much two missionaries who are willing to sacrifice and go the extra mile can change someone's life.

While on a visit with some good friends in Trollhattan, Sweden I received a copy of the Book of Mormon. They gave it to me just as I was getting ready to leave home. During the coming summer I read it during every opportunity that I had. It was strange, every time that I read in the Book of Mormon I felt something that I couldn't understand. I began to feel driven to continue reading this book. I really began to think a lot about what I was reading. My family and I lived in Kiruna, Sweden — there aren't any missionaries there — so during that time I was reading the Book of Mormon I didn't have any contact with the church.

Several months later I was talking with my relatives and the conversation turned to religion. One relative from Lulea told that she had received a visit from two well groomed young boys from the Mormon Church. When I heard that I told them that I had read the Book of Mormon. They tried to warn me about reading it, but I told them what I felt as I read it. I told them that it was the word of God exactly like the Bible was. My relative from Lulea told all about my proclamation to the missionaries during their next visit with her.

After a few days I received a letter from Lulea. It was from the missionaries who wanted to know if they could visit us in Kiruna (360 Kilometers north of Lulea). We wrote that they were welcome to come. The first discussion we talked about the restoration. I loved hearing about how Christ was the cornerstone and that the church today has a prophet and 12 apostles exactly as it was during the time when Christ was on the earth. Those thoughts went directly in my heart, I felt that this was exactly like Christ's Church should be.

During the next discussion the missionaries explained that all, ALL, who asked God would receive knowledge that the Book of Mormon is true. I had never really thought about that, but that night I thought that I would ask God. I believed that it would be a simple process. I had been taught about how I should pray. Before I went to bed that night I began to pray. I didn't get an answer! I tried again — and waited — nothing happened. I continued with prayer — my prayer became more intensive and serious, but still no answer — at least no answer that I could recognize. I wasn't going to give up, even though I began to be a bit confused. I began to think, If God had promised all which asked why hadn't he answered my question. Was I not worthy enough to receive an answer? Many thoughts went through my mind. I prayed for an answer during the entire night. About five in the morning something began to happen. I became warm throughout my entire body. I received an undescribable strong feeling within me. My words can't describe how I felt. Then, in the early morning time I received knowledge from our Heavenly Father that the Book of Mormon is true. I had received my answer.

I was filled with a strong feeling of joy. God had talked to me! Not a voice which you hear with your ears, but it was a feeling within me, the spirit talking to my spirit. I can never forget that feeling which I received that time. I felt prepared to do what I knew was true. The only thing I knew about members was that they didn't drink coffee. The first thing I said to my husband the next morning was that I now knew that which the missionaries told us about the Church was true and I wasn't going to drink any more coffee. Since that day I have never had coffee again. My husband wanted me to wait a while before I became baptized, so I waited 8 months. But on the day I was baptized finally it was a heavenly experience.

I love the Gospel. I am thankful for the missionaries which took the initiative and traveled 360 kilometers each way to teach me the Gospel.

Family Members

You should write home to your parents every week. Other correspondence should be limited. You should not call friends or family while in the mission field. Exceptions should be cleared in advance with the mission president.

Writing home every week will bring many blessings to your family. Not only are they concerned about your welfare, but your letters will have a positive influence on your home. As your family reads your letters, they will feel the Spirit. As you bear your testimony each week, their testimonies will also grow. As you talk of teaching the law of tithing or the Word or

Wisdom or the law of chastity, they will have even greater motivation to keep those commandments. And younger brothers and sisters will want to follow your example and prepare for their own missions. Many inactive or non-member parents have joined or become active in the Church through the missionary letters of their faithful sons and daughters.

Though writing home once a week will bring you and your family great blessings, writing more than that can prove distracting. Experience has shown that missionaries who are homesick for their families or friends become even more homesick when they receive an inordinate amount of letters from home.

A particular companion of mine was a strain on our companionship. This Elder helped me to realize just how a companionship needs to work. He had a girlfriend who would send him a tape every week. There is nothing wrong with sending tapes, but every week this Elder would hoard this tape and listen to it when it was time for bed at night. It was 10:30 p.m. and we all wanted to go to sleep, and then he'd turn on his tape. He'd put the covers over his head and stick the tape player next to his ear. I didn't laugh, although I thought it was kind of funny at first. Then I started noticing that at 11:00 p.m., 12:00 a.m., and 1:30 a.m. he was still listening to these tapes over and over and over again. I asked him to quit doing it. I said, "Hey, if you want to listen to these things, listen to them in the shower or somewhere like that." Listening long into the night became a habit for him, and in the mornings he could hardly drag himself out of bed. He would be extremely tired all day, and his excitement in life was listening to these tapes every night. He would continue to listen to them over and over and over. Finally a good visit from a district leader, who wanted to know what he was doing under the sheets at 1:00 a.m. stopped it all. Our mission president wrote to his girlfriend and asked her to stop sending the tapes. The tapes weren't really the thing that was bad, but it was the way this Elder was letting them affect him. Always remember that it's a companionship. The companionship has to be two ways. If you are destroying your companion's sleep, you need to stop what you're doing. If you are bothering your companion, you need to stop it. A true companionship is just like a marriage; you have to think of each other more than yourself.

Members of the Opposite Sex

As a missionary you should never be alone with or have correspondence with anyone of the opposite sex within your mission boundaries.

Single investigators of the opposite sex should be taught only in the presence of an adult member of the Church. You should not live in apartments or homes where single people of the opposite sex reside, unless your mission president gives his specific approval.

The attention you are receiving from a member of the opposite sex many be totally innocent. But others will not see it that way. And even innocent attention can turn to something stronger. So please, keep up the barrier of reserve between you and members of the opposite sex. There will be plenty of time after your mission for dating and courtship. Now is not the time.

Companions

We have discussed the close, helpful relationship that should exist between missionary companions. As mentioned, missionary companions should never be separated. They must always stay together. And that means staying *close* together, not merely within sight of one another or in the same building. Don't make any exceptions.

Avoid situations that can lead to trouble or that can take on the appearance of evil.

Please read: Thessalonians 5:22 and Proverbs 4:14-15.

As these scriptures suggest, avoid even the appearance of evil, turn away from it, shun it.

Trust in the Lord and not your own strength.

As mentioned before, you may think you can handle teaching members of the opposite sex alone. But sad experiences have shown that every missionary who is sent home for transgression always thought he had the strength to withstand temptation in the beginning. The best way to withstand temptation is to avoid it. And even if you are strong enough to resist temptation, think of others who might not be. Think of your companion, or the missionaries who will replace you. You owe it to them to avoid temptation and the appearance of evil as you would avoid a deadly disease that you knew you could not withstand.

The Lord has promised to be on your right hand, on your left hand, and to go before you at all times. But the Holy Ghost will only be your constant companion as long as you desire his companionship. If you willingly enter into morally or physically dangerous situations, then the Lord may not protect you. Your free agency is still very much in force as a missionary. You can make choices that will bless others and yourself, or you can choose to do that which will harm others and yourself. The choice is still yours — make it the right one.

Joseph Smith said: "I teach them correct principles, and they govern themselves." (As quoted by John Taylor, *Millennial Star,* 13:339.) You now know what great expectations the Lord has for you. But you will quickly find that there is no one to constantly look over your shoulder and supervise your work. Perhaps for the first time in your life you will be governing yourself. To be certain, you have some very specific guidelines to follow. But no one is there to enforce them. Your obedience, success, and happiness rest squarely on your's and your companion's shoulders.

How you act when you are on your own tells much about who you really are.

Please read and memorize D & C 4.

This is really a missionary's code of conduct and formula for success. Don't just memorize this scripture — live it.

There are missionaries who constantly fight all of their mission's rules. And there are missionaries who give so much attention to mission rules that they miss the whole point of the freedoms each discipline is supposed to bring.

Make up your mind to live each mission rule to the letter and with the Spirit. If you make sure to always be in bed by 10:30 at night, when the exception comes you will know it. You will certainly encounter mission rules that are a sacrifice for you to keep. For example, you may be the only missionary in your mission who finds it a challenge to write home every week. But if you will give up something good, then the Lord will open up opportunities to you that you would not have if you had been disobedient. In other words, if you will give up something good, He will give you something better.

I have a testimony that the Lord will bless you if you keep his laws. It's really as simple as that.

Elder William R. Bradford has said this, concerning the sanctifying power of disciplined missionary work:

This is a marvelous plan. It is a process of sanctification. When a missionary is placed in a mission environment of order and discipline where all that is done is in harmony with the Spirit, the missionary experiences a great transformation. The heavens open. Powers are showered out. mysteries are revealed. Habits are improved.

Sanctification begins. Through this process the missionary becomes a vessel of light that can shine forth the gospel of Jesus Christ in a world in darkness. (William R. Bradford, *Ensign*, November 1982, p. 51.)

Your personal righteousness and spirituality will greatly affect your mission and the lives of thousands of people you meet. I have seen missionaries who are sensitive to the Spirit bring about striking, positive changes in the lives of individuals and families. You can do the same. I know you can. But learning how is up to you.

Challenge

Read "Mission Policy," in the *Missionary Handbook*, pages 9-17.

Chapter 3

The Discussions

He conquers who endures.

Persius

Nothing in the world can take the
place of persistence. Talent will not;
nothing is more common than unsuccessful
men with talent. Genius will not;
unrewarded genius is almost a proverb.·
Education will not; the world is full of
educated derelicts. Persistence and
determination alone are omnipotent.

Calvin Coolidge

Scriptures:
D & C 66:9-13, D & C 106: 6-8

Elder Jim
Vancouver, BC Mission

My first day in the mission field. After months of looking forward to it, the preparation, the shopping, the goodbyes, the spirit-swelling, brain-straining weeks at the MTC, and there I was. I was met at the airport by my mission president and two other missionaries. Their warm smiles and hearty welcome quickly dissipated the nervousness that had found its way into the hollow of my stomach.

I was taken from the airport to the mission office and given some supplies, along with some mail addressed to a guy that I found out was to be my first companion. I tried to imagine what he'd be like. The mission president took me into his office and told me how glad he was to have me in his mission and showed me on the map where my first area was to be. I wondered if he could tell how scared I was.

The same blue van that brought us to the office then took us to the mission home. After meeting the mission president's wife, I started to somehow feel that I just might make it after all. We had barely been introduced, and I was already peeling potatoes for the evening's dinner. After dinner, I spent some time in an interview with the president and then it was off to bed. The day's events, however, had happened much too fast for my mind to allow my body to get any sleep.

The next morning, I found myself back in the blue van, heading to something they called a ferry terminal. Before I knew it, my luggage and I had been whisked down the dock and onto the ferry, which was now departing for shores unknown. My companion was to meet me on the other side. Once there, there was only time for exchanging an enthusiastic handshake and tossing the luggage in the trunk, because we had a short amount of time to drive the distance between there and the next ferry we were to take. We spent the next couple of hours getting to know each other as we drove towards my first area. He was a super guy, and I could tell that we were going to get along great.

As we neared our area he mentioned that we had two discussions that night. I said, "Great", and he said, "Yeah, we meet our splits at 7:00." "Splits?" As he explained it to me, I was to go with one of the local ward members to teach one discussion and he would go with another to teach a second discussion, since they were both scheduled at the same time. I tried to explain to my companion that there was one flaw in his plan: I had just come from the MTC the day before and had never given a real live discussion before. He said there was no other way to do it and that I would go to teach a first discussion to a family that had never been taught before. At least that way I had a fair shot at remembering most of the discussion since we had covered it pretty thoroughly in the MTC, and, at any rate, the family wouldn't have any basis of comparison.

Talk about sweating! I couldn't believe the fix I was in. I had been sort of counting on sliding by on my companion's knowledge for the first little while. The thought of going solo on my first day out scared me to death. I girded up my loins as best I could and resolved to give it my best shot.

My split arrived, and we drove to the family's house. They were a married couple in their late twenties. They seemed really nice, especially the wife. Little did I know of the ordeal that was lying in wait for me. The husband fancied himself an intellectual and had gathered a large amount of anti-Mormon material. He had taken one book in particular that consisted of questions that were designed to lead a missionary into an inescapable trap, and he had copied the questions down into a notebook to make it look like they were his questions. The wife, it turned out, had developed a very serious case of diabetes and was not expected to survive it for very much longer. She had received a Book of Mormon and some pamphlets from a sister of hers who had been converted to the Church some years earlier. This sister was very concerned that the woman join the Church before she passed away. She had become very interested in the Church and had felt the Holy Ghost as she studied about it. It was in opposition to this interest that her husband had accumulated all of the anti-Mormon material and had arranged for the missionaries to come over so he could discredit them.

I'm not sure that I could have handled just a simple discussion, and I certainly wasn't ready for all that this man hit me with. I was just a nineteen year old kid and I hadn't been a member of the Church too long myself, so much of what he said I couldn't even understand, let alone answer. The man hit me with things like the Adam-God theory and the King Follet sermon and other things I had never heard of. Before long, I was completely befuddled. Any attempt I made to deliver what little of the discussion I could remember was thwarted by his relentless badgering. So there I was, my back was against the wall and he was closing in for the kill. While I was still reeling from one assault, he relentlessly launched another. "How come you Mormons don't believe in blood transfusions?" I was stumped. He had mixed us up with the Jehovah's Witnesses, but being a recent convert, I was not familiar enough with our own doctrines to know that. I couldn't figure out for the life of me why Joseph Smith would say something against blood transfusions. I, myself, had donated blood many times before I joined the Church. I had prayed and gained a testimony of the restored Gospel, though, and I knew that whatever it taught was the truth. I realized that I wasn't going to get anywhere with this man by trying to find answers to his many accusations. Battle-weary and a little overwhelmed, but still holding fast to my testimony, I looked at this man and his wife, and I said, "Sir, I'm not sure why our church doesn't believe in blood transfusions. In fact, there's a lot I probably don't know about this church. I sat where you're sitting not much more than a year ago. When the missionaries taught me, there were things I couldn't understand and there were things I had a hard time accepting, but I couldn't deny the feelings I was having. The Holy Ghost filled my heart, and I began to develop a testimony. I somehow knew that what I didn't then know, I didn't have to worry about. It would all come in time. I heard someone say, and I don't know if it was a scripture or a song, that we would learn the Gospel line upon line, precept upon precept. I wasn't really sure what that meant when I first heard it, but I'm starting to understand it now. This Gospel has changed my life, and I know it can change yours. What a tragedy it would be to throw it away just because you can't see it all right now. I know that Joseph Smith was a prophet of God, and if we don't believe in blood transfusions, then I testify to you that it's a true principle."

There I was, bearing testimony of something that wasn't even true, but the Spirit was there. The woman was in tears, and she began to plead with her husband to let her be baptized. I think that because she was so close to the veil, with her impending death, that she was especially sensitive to the Spirit. Her husband, however, remained unmoved. He forbad her to be baptized, and he asked me to leave.

I have thought often of that first night in the mission field and of that sweet woman. I have no doubt but that the good Lord took care of her when she arrived on the other side of the veil. I learned then that as we go out teaching the Gospel to the world, it is not the Church, or the Book of Mormon, or Joseph Smith that is on trial, it is the people to whom we bring the Gospel message.

●   ●   ●

You may not know it, but the missionary discussions have not been around all that long. In the old days missionaries often had no uniform method for teaching families. But today's missionaries are able to use an excellent and very concise format for teaching the gospel — the proselyting discussions.

Learning how to use these discussions is essential to becoming an effective teacher of the gospel. You will note that each discussion has a main concept with several supporting concepts. Most of your teaching will evolve around the presentation of these concepts. Although you should be able to teach the entire discussion alone, usually you and your companion will trade off between concepts, which helps your investigators keep interested and allows both of you to be involved in the teaching process. It also gives your voice a rest. Also note that with each concept is a list of precepts and examples that can be used to answer questions an investigator might have. These are very important. Some missionaries concentrate so heavily on memorizing the concepts that they neglect to study the supporting doctrines and teachings. But to really use the discussions as they were intended, you should become familiar with every sentence in the discussions, paying equal attention to the teaching skills.

At the end of each discussion you will commit your investigators to follow a specific course of action, as they contemplate what you have said and read specific reading assignments. The beauty of the discussions is that they prepare people with small commitments in the beginning which lead to larger commitments. Your investigators won't usually be challenged to quit smoking and pay tithing on the first discussion.

The discussions help people grow and also prepare people for membership. To help prepare "active" members there needs to be commitment. The gospel is a gospel of commitment; the Celestial Kingdom is not arrived at by accident. At the end of each discussion, you will also set an appointment for the next discussion. Afterwards you will follow up on each discussion by reconfirming the appointment in a day or two, or having a friendshipper drop by on the investigators.

How can you do this? Practice. Practice going through the discussions with your companion, role-playing an investigator who has reservations about certain doctrines of the Church. If you will become familiar with this supporting material, then you will be much better prepared to help an investigator understand difficult precepts, such as the importance of baptism by one with authority or the law of tithing. You will find that some portions of the discussions ask you to give an example or teach a certain concept in your own words. Make the time to memorize several examples that you can utilize in these sections. With several examples ever ready, you will be prepared to select the one that is most appropriate for the investigators you are teaching.

While you should learn some parts of the discussion word-for-word, you may find yourself getting stuck on the wording on one particular phrase. If so, then simply rephrase it so that you can be more comfortable in presenting its ideas. The problem of wording can be particularly difficult when teaching in a foreign language. You must understand exactly what you are saying before you attempt to teach it. If you are uncomfortable with a particular grammatical construction, then have an experienced missionary or member help you with it. A word of caution: When you do rephrase a sentence, be careful not to change its meaning or emphasis.

The missionary discussions are an important tool in teaching the gospel. But don't forget that the discussions are really just an vehicle for us to prepare investigators for teaching and conversion by the Holy Ghost.

Don't get upset if everyone doesn't recognize the Holy Ghost's influence immediately. All investigators may not be as interested and as "golden" as others. Missionaries need to be able to do more than simply teach discussions to be effective. They need to be able to answer questions and handle the investigator's concerns.

At the Missionary Training Center, you will learn several teaching skills to help you do this effectively. You might try practicing with a friend or someone in your family the section in the lesson titled "Invite to Pray."

"Invite to Pray" means just what it says. When an investigator is having difficulty, a missionary may encourage him to pray to God to obtain understanding or strength. This is a very effective teaching skill which was used many times in the scriptures. For a scriptural example of an invitation to pray refer to, Alma 22:15-18, and see how Aaron invited Lamoni's father to pray.

Imagine if you were teaching someone and he had just told you that he can't accept the Joseph Smith story because he finds it hard to believe in angels and things like that. You, as the missionary, could respond: "I'm sure it is a little difficult to accept something like that. But there is a way to find out if it's true. If you will get down on your knees and ask your Father in Heaven about Joseph Smith, I promise you that He will tell you whether or not Joseph saw God. Will you pray about it?" This is an example of using the "Invite to Pray" skill.

If you are going to role-play with a friend or member of your family, try to make this exercise as serious as possible. Try, though, not to be overly skeptical or reluctant. The purpose of this exercise is to practice giving the discussion, not to give each other a hard time.

At this time do *not* attempt to memorize the discussion. Simply follow along in your mission package as you present it.

Challenge

Obtain a copy of the current missionary discussions and completely read through them as soon as you can. Remember that the discussions are only the beginning of the teaching process. Become a well rounded missionary. As you go through the discussions, attempt to anticipate questions that your investigators will ask. Spend some time now in gospel study answering those potential questions. Be prepared when that golden family asks something important to them to give a well thought out answer backed with a strong personal testimony of the truthfulness of the Gospel of Jesus Christ.

Chapter 4

Finding People to Teach

Nothing happens by itself . . . It all
will come your way, once you understand
that you have to make it come your
way, by your exertions.

Ben Stein

Scriptures:
Alma Chapter 17, Romans 1:16, Luke 18:29,30, D & C 84: 80,85

Elder Hunter
England, London Mission

> *At the first of my mission, I must admit, I was somewhat less*
> *than enthusiastic about tracting and street contacting. I had always*
> *been rather shy, and the thought of approaching complete strangers*
> *about the Gospel terrified me. I was willing to teach them, but let*
> *someone else go find them. It wasn't long before I decided that I must*
> *surely hate door-knocking more than any other missionary in the*
> *mission. I even remember faking ringing the doorbell when it was my*
> *door a couple of times. When I approached my companion about my*
> *problem, he suggested a rather dramatic remedy. He proposed that*

since I hated tracting more than any other missionary, I should therefore do more tracting than any other missionary. This wasn't exactly the solution I was hoping for, but since he was the senior I decided to give it a try. What followed was something quite amazing that I still can't explain. For the next few weeks we tracted practically all the time. By the end of each day my feet would be killing me. We more than doubled the mission minimums for tracting each week. Somewhere in all those slammed doors and sore muscles, I developed a love for tracting. Some of my greatest mission memories are of pounding the streets of England with my companions and of our many doorstep escapades. When I look back on the people that I was able to teach and baptize, on the precious relationships that I developed with investigators and converts, I realize that many of them were a result of door-knocking. This success was possible because of our attitude towards the work and our willingness to do it.

Throughout my mission I learned from the great examples of other missionaries. One of the greatest examples still stands out in my mind. I was assigned as a zone leader to a zone that had not been having a great deal of success. On the same transfer day several other missionaries were brought fresh into the zone. After a few weeks I started getting reports from one of my district leaders about a missionary in his district. At that time, we were required to get statistics from each companionship at the end of every week. This particular missionary, it seems, was reporting statistics that were fantastically high. In an area that had been all but dead for a long time, this missionary was claiming to be teaching over forty discussions in a week, including fifteen to twenty first discussions. In addition, this missionary's companion was complaining to the district leader that he was being forced to tract too much. I decided to arrange a split so I could check the situation out. I swapped companions with this missionary for a day, and what followed was one of the most amazing days of my mission. When I got to this missionary's area, I discovered that he really did have at least twenty people that he was helping to progress towards baptism, and all of them came from tracting. Before we left the apartment that morning, I asked him how he could possibly have that much success tracting. What he said literally changed my mission. He replied, "I don't go out to knock on doors; I go out to teach. Anybody can knock on doors, but I figure I don't have time for that. I tell myself when I go out that I am going out to teach. That way, instead of knocking on doors just because I have to get so many hours of door-knocking in, I knock on doors so I can teach. When I approach a door, I pause for a second just before I knock, and in that second I tell myself that I have an appointment there. It's all in the attitude."

Sure enough, we taught four new first discussions that day, in addition to teaching discussions to about five or six other people that he had found the week before. While we were tracting, we literally ran from door to door. I felt a sense of urgency about the work, and a pervading desire to teach gripped my heart. We ended up having to bring in an additional pair of missionaries to help with the teaching of the investigators this missionary was finding. As it turned out, after two months of twelve and fifteen baptisms, respectively, this missionary was forced to go home because of an existing illness that none of us knew about. He knew that his time in the mission field might be limited, and I guess that's why he refused to waste a minute of it.

I learned a lot from that experience that I was able to apply not only to my mission but also to my life after my mission. That missionary was successful in finding people to teach because he had an overwhelming desire to baptize and he was willing to work as hard as necessary to fulfill that desire. I learned that a good many of life's battles are won or lost before they're ever fought, depending on a person's attitude.

•   •   •

If you are going to teach people the gospel, you will first have to find people who will listen to your message. You can find them yourself or with the help of members. The member method of finding is much to be preferred.

You will find your success increases tremendously as you learn to work closely with members of the Church to find investigators. Members of the Church are so successful because they have already created interest in the Church by their unique lifestyle and high standard of living. They have also established a foundation of trust with their non-member friends and associates that would take many months for missionaries to establish. Statistics show that one in one thousand persons contacted by the missionaries eventually joins the Church. In contrast, one out of five persons contacted by members joins the Church. And one out of three persons contacted by members and taught in the member's home joins the Church.

Although you are a full-time missionary, ideally most of your time should be spent teaching the gospel to investigators that the members have found. Really, missionary work is the responsibility of the members. You are to be a resource (a specialist) to help them teach the gospel to their friends and families. When you talk to the members about missionary work, project the attitude of a willful servant who would like to help them with their missionary responsibilities.

Consider some of the following scriptures, which place the responsibility of finding investigators onto the Church member:

1. D & C 88:81 — *Every man who has been warned should warn his neighbor* — All members of the Church enjoy tremendous blessings and happiness because of their knowledge of the gospel. We have an obligation to share this happiness with others.

2. D & C 38:40-42 — *Every member should preach the gospel* — All of us have been commanded to go forth and labor with our might to bring the gospel to others. We are to be as a voice crying in the wilderness.

3. Mosiah 18:9 — *At baptism we promise to stand as witnesses at all times, in all places* — At our baptism we promised to bear witness of the gospel and to shoulder all the responsibilities of members of Christ's church.

There are two keys to productive missionary work — (1) family to family friendshipping (when a member family shares the gospel with a nonmember family), and (2) cooperation between members and the missionaries to teach people.

It is impractical for us to expect that . . . missionaries alone can warn the millions in the world. Members must be finders. The valuable time of our teaching missionaries is too often spent in 'finding.'

Members should shoulder this responsibility. Every member knows of nonmembers he or she can refer to the missionaries. Every father, mother, and youth in this Church should share the gospel by giving a Book of Mormon, telling the account of the Prophet Joseph Smith, or inviting our acquaintances to a special meeting. If we are in tune, the Spirit of the Lord will speak to us and guide us to those with whom we should share to gospel. The Lord will help us if we will but listen.

It is the responsibility of the members to provide the stake and full-time missionaries with the names of individuals and families to teach. Sometimes we forget that it is better to risk a little ruffling in the relationship of a friend than it is to deprive him of eternal life by keeping silent. (Spencer W. Kimball, Address delivered at Regional Representatives Seminar, 3 Apr. 1975.)

Members of the Church often know many people who are ready to hear the gospel. The problem is members are often reluctant to approach their acquaintances about the gospel. You can help them overcome this reluctance by:

• Being the kind of missionary the members will trust with their nonmember family and friends.

• Asking members about acquaintances who may be interested in the gospel.

- Ask members to choose someone to share the gospel with.

- Teach members how to friendship.

- Follow through on referrals and report back to the members regarding how you were received.

While your own love and interest in investigators is important, it is absolutely essential that people who are investigating the Church find friends within the local branch or ward. Members are much better friend-shippers that are missionaries. There are several reasons for this. First, members will be around long after the missionaries who taught the investigators the gospel have gone home. Members have interests and concerns similar to those of investigators (such as local politics, schools, raising families, keeping within a budget, etc.). They also can engage in similar activities (such as going to concerts, movies, dances, etc.). In addition, members know the needs of investigators better than do missionaries and can help investigators feel more comfortable socially when they attend Church.

Obtain a copy of the brochure *I Need a Friend.* You can get one through your ward or stake mission leader.

Here are a few friendshipping ideas which you can pass along to members:

- Invite non-member friends and acquaintances to a special family home evening.

- Invite your children's non-member friends to primary (be sure to get their parents' permission first).

- Invite older non-member youth to church activities or to partici-pate in Church plays and road shows.

- If possible, take non-member friends to your local temple's visitor's center.

- Invite friends over for movies or dinner.

Please remember that even if the members' friends do not choose to learn more about the Church, their friendship will still be important to the members. Should you at some point become involved with members' friends and then find that they are no longer interested in learning more about the Church, then allow them to make that decision without pressure or embarrassment. Perhaps in future months their hearts will change as they ponder the principles they have observed and been taught.

Sometime members will give you a referral and then expect you to carry the work forward from there. But members must stay involved in teaching the gospel to their friends. Indeed, it is their example and testimony that has such a winning influence with their friends. You can keep the members involved in numerous ways. For example, you may want to ask members to arrange for the gospel to be taught in their homes. Once you start teaching the discussions, you should ask them to keep in daily contact with their friends to help their friends understand precepts with which they may be struggling. You should also ask them to bring their friends to worship services and activities. Explain to members that their presence will help their friends feel more comfortable while receiving the gospel and that the member's testimony and friendship usually have great impact on non-members willingness to accept challenges to pray or to attend church.

When you find investigators on your own, then try immediately to involve members in the teaching process. You can do this by bringing a member with you to the next discussion. Before the meeting with the investigator(s), ask the member to offer to bring the investigator to church. Once the investigator is at church, introduce them to the bishop or branch president and other leaders. Also make sure to introduce them to members of the ward or branch who live close to them. And then get several different members to invite them to church activities. Always keep your eyes open for ways to involve members in your (their) work.

You will find in your efforts to help members with their missionary work that some members might be afraid to approach friends or family about the gospel. You can help them overcome their shyness by involving them in the friendshipping of one of your investigators. You can also role-play some proselyting or teaching situations with them. Once they see how much fun missionary work can be they can quickly overcome their inhibitions. Often members who were once the most timid about sharing the gospel become top member-missionaries in their ward or branch. They made that change because some missionaries took the time to help them in their missionary duties.

On one occasion in the branch where I was serving, we instituted a co-tracting program. We started scheduling several times a week for members to go out tracting with the missionaries. We figured that much more could be accomplished with four people than with just two. After a while we were accomplishing more than double what we normally would have, so we continued to do this. One day my companion was out with a member tracting, and they knocked on a door. The lady who answered was totally unresponsive. The lady looked familiar to the member with the Elder, so he said, "Haven't I seen you somewhere?" She said, "Yes, I've seen you at the store." This started a little conversation about the store and shopping, and before they knew it they were invited in. The member created the warmth and the friendship which got the return invitation, not the missionary. The missionary was used from that point on to teach, and the lady was baptized. Missionary efforts can be doubled with the use of members.

Finding People Through Investigators and Part-Member Families

Many missionaries have had success obtaining referrals and help from investigators and contacts. And many successful contacts have been made by inviting the investigator's family and friends to the baptismal service or to discussion visits. When appropriate, try to get referrals after every discussion you teach.

As you teach non-members the gospel, ask them if they have family, friends or neighbors who might be interested in your message. Often investigators can find many people who have a desire for the gospel. If investigators can get their family and friends interested, then some good things will happen. First, more people will be introduced to the teachings of the gospel. Second, your investigators will be discussing the gospel with others who have also been taught the gospel. This discussion will bring the Spirit. And it is the Spirit who converts. Third, investigators will have more social reinforcement when they attend church and are less likely to meet resistance from family and friends if they, too, have been taught the gospel.

You should encourage investigators who are progressing towards baptism to be open with friends and family about their plans to join the Church. Although they quite likely will encounter opposition from those close to them, this opposition is not necessarily bad. When family or friends oppose an investigator's joining the Church, it often has the effect of causing the investigator to think and pray more deeply about the commitment he is about to make. This often strengthens their conviction. And it prepares them for further opposition as they continue their activity in the Church. It is a strange phenomenon, but it seems that whenever someone wants to join the Church their friends and family suddenly object. What is especially peculiar is that often the person joining the Church has adopted a lifestyle friends or family really approve of (such as giving up smoking, drinking, swearing, or unchastity).

Another reason investigators should be open about their plans is that an open, confident expression of their fledgling testimonies can often spark a desire in their family and friends to learn more about the gospel. It can also put an early halt to opposition.

Working with part-member families is also an effective way of finding and preparing people to be taught. This has the double advantage of strengthening the members as well as converting the nonmembers in the family. In every area missionaries should regularly review the entire ward list with local priesthood leaders. With their priesthood leaders' permission, visit the homes of part-member families and establish a rapport with them.

While a hundred missionaries may have tried with this particular part-member family, you may be the one to convert the person who isn't a member. Go with the Spirit of love and friendship. Say,"I'm new in this area." Sometimes people like the idea that you are new, and that you don't know about their past mistakes. Just be a friend to them.

You should be certain to coordinate all missionary efforts (in both part-member and non-member households) with the father. By showing respect for his leadership you can create a feeling of trust and keep harmony within the home.

Finding People Through Personal Contacting

The responsibility to find people to teach is primarily the members' but missionaries are also charged to seek out and gather in the elect. (See D & C 75:18-19; 111:2-3.) They should take advantage of every opportunity to talk with people about the gospel.

Missionaries shouldn't be afraid to approach people. The Lord promises to bless those who, with humility, have the courage to proclaim his message.

Please read the following scriptures: Acts 18:9-11, D & C 112:19 and D & C 100:56.

The Lord promises to be with you and to lead you in what you say and do if you will be obedient and trust in Him.

President Gordon B. Hinkley tells this story about being lead by the Lord:

I was on a mission in England. I had been called to labor in the European Mission office in London under President Joseph F. Merrill of the Council of the Twelve, then president of the European Mission. One day three or four of the London papers carried reviews of a reprint of an old book, snide and ugly in tone, indicating that the book was a history of the Mormons. President Merrill said to me, 'I want you to go down to the publisher and protest this.' I looked at him and was about to say, 'Surely not me.' But I meekly said, 'Yes, sir.'

I do not hesitate to say that I was frightened. I went to my room and felt something as I think Moses must have felt when the Lord asked him to go and see Pharaoh. I offered a prayer. My stomach was churning as I walked over to the Goodge Street station to get the underground train to Fleet Street. I found the office of the president and presented my card to the receptionist. She took it and went into the inner office and soon returned to say that Mr. Skeffington was too busy to see me. I replied that I had come five thousand miles and that I would wait. During the next hour she made two or three trips to his office, then finally invited me in. I shall never forget the picture when I entered. He was smoking a long cigar with a look that seemed to say, 'Don't bother me.'

I held in my hand the reviews. I do not know what I said after that. Another power seemed to be speaking through me. At first he was defensive and even belligerent. Then he began to soften. He concluded by promising to do something. Within an hour word went out to every book dealer in England to return the books to the publisher. At great expense he printed and tipped in the front of each volume a statement to the effect that the book was not to be considered as history, but only as fiction, and that no offense was intended against the respected Mormon people. Years later he granted another favor of substantial worth to the Church, and each year until the time of his death I received a Christmas card from him.

I came to know that when we try in faith to walk in obedience to the requests of the priesthood, the Lord opens the way, even when there appears to be no way. (Gordon B. Hinckley, *Ensign*, Dec. 1971, pp. 124-25.)

There are various methods of meeting people and introducing them to the gospel. Here are some of the better known ways:

- Door-to door tracting;

- Setting up a street display and contacting people going to or from work or shopping

- Giving presentations to professional groups,

- Service organizations, and clubs

- Inviting people to "Mormon Nights" featuring General Authorities or LDS celebrities, or to local pageants or road shows

- Using Church-produced films and filmstrips;

- Contacting the local news media regarding missionary-related special events, programs or just about your mission. (I had a lot of fun doing this).

- Talking to people wherever you go about the gospel. That includes talking to people on trains, buses, at the barber or hair-dresser, and at the post office. Once you get the hang of this it is really fun.

- Teaching about LDS history and culture in local high schools and colleges.

- Preparation day sporting events within the confines of mission rules.

The point is, you have to meet people face-to-face and get them interested in the message of the gospel.

"What, *me* contact people face-to-face?"

Yes, you. If you have not been an extrovert until now (and few of us have been), then your life is about to change. By extrovert I don't mean a show-off or an overbearing, stop-me-if-you-can-get-a-word-in egotist. But rather what I mean is that you must be bold in declaring the gospel.

Do you have the courage to try business contacting? How do you feel interrupting a tired laborer's night in front of the TV? Can you approach the principal of a high school and offer to present yourselves to the student body, to a group of young people just one or two years younger than yourselves? Can you drop in on a busy news editor and tell him about your mission and suggest that he devote his precious editorial space to a story or two about you and your companion? Can you stand up on a bench in a park or on a crowded busy street and preach a sermon?

The answer is that you can. Oh, I know the thought of it makes you cringe. But that is because you have not learned how much fun it can be. And before I share some personal examples of successful person-to-person contacting, let me list a few of the benefits you will receive if you will let go of your inhibitions, and with a leap of faith, openly declare the gospel of Jesus Christ.

• Personal contacting helps you develop communication skills that you can use throughout your life.

• It helps you develop interpersonal skills and a confidence in working with people.

• It helps develop courage and strong character.

• It allows you to get a better understanding of the people in the area.

Using Your Imagination

One of the fun parts of my mission involved going beyond the routine of just knocking on doors. I had fun going and doing some public relations. Every missionary is a unique commodity. The newspapers absolutely love stories on missionary nut cases who go out when they are nineteen or twenty. Early in my mission I started talking with a reporter and before I knew it we had a two page article about the church and Joseph Smith that was very complimentary. We did that again and again. The way to get an article in the paper is just pure guts. Dress professionally, put together a few brochures on Christ, along with any other articles you may have, then walk into the office, and ask to speak to the head editor. Sit down and tell the editor that you have a very interesting article for them. If you are in Spokane, Washington, or Hong Kong, missionaries make local paper news. Knocking on doors you will maybe reach a hundred people, but through a newspaper you will reach a thousand. Get the reporter to include information about Joseph Smith, clear up some misconceptions about the Church, maybe interview a local member, and if possible have them print your telephone number or address where they can contact you either directly or through your mission office. The following are four of my favorite articles that we got in local areas where I was working or visiting as a missionary. The best part is that each article excited the members, made a lot of friends in the community, dispelled a lot of bad information in the communities and led to many people letting us in for discussions who normally wouldn't have. But, most importantly, they led to conversions.

Examples of Free Publicity

Called to Serve

ONSDAGEN DEN 15 OKTOBER 1975 KT 5

KARLSKOGA

Marc Garrison och Steve Brown kom till Karlskoga i fredags. De är missionärer inom Jesu Kristi Kyrka av Sista Dagars Heliga.

Mormoner från Amerika missionerar i Karlskoga

Marc och Steve, båda amerikaner, träffades första gången i fredags. De gjorde det i Karlskoga, där de båda ska verka som missionärer. De är mormoner, och är utsända av sin kyrka att missionera i Sverige. De är unga, de har båda avbrutit sina universitetsstudier för att under ett par år verka ute på missionsfältet.

De kommer att »knacka dörr» i Karlskoga och Degerfors. Marc Stephen Garrison stannar i ett halvår framöver, medan James Steven Brown kommer att resa från och till.

Det finns församling i Karlskoga. Jesu Kristi kyrka av Sista Dagars Heliga har samlingslokal på Ekeby. Där har man söndagsskola. För gudstjänster åker man till Örebro.

Medlem i Jesu Kristi Kyrka av Sista Dagars Heliga kallas mormoner. Rörelsen uppkom inte ur någon oenighet med annan kristen livsåskådning, utan kom på 1830-talet genom profeten Joseph Smith.

Så berättar Marc och Steve. De presenterar sin kyrka som

en samlingsplats för alla yrkesgrupper, för män och kvinnor, för alla åldrar. Det finns tre miljoner, spridda runt hela världen, men med en dominans i Amerika.

De grundläggande mormonlärdomarna är tro på Gud Fadern, Jesus Kristus och Den Helige Anden.

— Vi tror på att människan är en evig varelse och vi tror på att livet har en mening, säger Marc och Steve.

Vi tror däremot inte på någon reinkarnation, inget Nirvana ingen statisk himmel eller ett helvete av heta lågor. Himlen finns i den tillväxt som kommer av att bli bättre och uppnå sina mål.

För många människor har mormonismen bara betytt en enda sak - nämligen månggifte. Före 1890 förekom det månggifte bland mormoner, men efter nämnda årtal, så har inga polygama vigslar förrättats.

Som mormon använder man inte sprit, tobak eller narkotika. Man dricker inte te eller kaffe heller. Men vi firar jul och fö-

delsedagar, vi tar emot blodöverföring och vi nekar inte att göra vår militärtjänstgöring.

Vi tror på vår religion och vi vill att andra ska få möjligheter att ta del av den. Därför går vi ut och missionerar, säger Marc och Steve, som själva betalar alla kostnader för sitt uppehälle och sin verksamhet i Sverige. De lever enkelt, de cyklar dit de ska och har båda skaffat sig begagnade cyklar. De kommer att knacka på hos människorna i de här trakterna runt Karlskoga. De tänker inte tvinga sig på hos någon, men är glada om man öppnar dörren och låter dem komma in och prata om Sista Dagars Heliga. De tycker om att träffa människor, och de tror att de kommer att lära sig mycket av sin vistelse i Sverige.

Innan de kom hit, så genomgick de en sju veckors utbildningstid. Då lärde man svenska bl.a. I dag kan de det nästan flytande. Marc har en dragning åt skånska, beroende på att han innan han kom till Karlskoga förra veckan tjänstgjort i Landskrona.

SIV GRIP

75

16 - NORDVÄSTSKÅNE

Unga mormoner cyklar runt med sitt budskap

DE MISSIONERAR I SVERIGE!

Av BENGT BROSTRÖM

LANDSKRONA: Landskroaborna ser dem ofta. De kommer trampande på sina cyklar, en lång och en kort kille, snyggt och oklanderligt klädda. Kanske väcker de förundran. Den vore säkert berättigad om det blev bekant, att de två ynglingarna är — missionärer!

, Varför ska man missionera i Sverige? Vi skickar ju missionärer till andra länder!

* Många har en tro. Andra har ingen alls. De här två, 19-årige amerikanerna, Marc Stephen Garrison och Robert H Russon, är ut sända av Jesu Kristi Kyrka av Sista Dagars Heliga. De är vad som populärt kallas mormoner. Och mormonerna har sökt värva nya själar för sin uppfattning sedan 125 år tillbaka. Till Sverige kom de första "missionärerna" i mitten av förra seklet.

■ FÖRSAKELSER

Det är med stora försakelser och uppoffringar, som de här ungdomarna — det finns 136 i hela Sverige — kommit för att missionera bland oss.

Marc Garrison började tänka på missionsuppdraget vid 16 år. Hans kamrat Robert H Russon är uppväxt i en mormonfamilj och har »sålede» missionsperioden att se fram emot »så länge han minns.

Efter studier och prov har de antts värdiga att bege sig ut i världen. De har sparat under många år. Familjen och vänner skjuter till pengar. Väl på plats får de klara sig själva. Till och med flygresan till Sverige har de delvis fått betala själva.

■ 500 KR MÅNAD

— Varje månad får vi 500 kr va. dera hemifrån. Det lever vi på, berättar Marc Garrison. Det går bra, förklarar han lite försynt.

Under två år är de borta från familjerna i Kalifornien resp Salt Lake City, mormon-huvudstaden. De skiftar uppehållsplats. Således har Garrison varit i Jönköping, medan Russon missionerat i Skellefteå, Umeå och Vänersborg tidigare.

De två anser sig ha haft tur som kom till Sverige. Vart de skulle sändas i världen visste de inte förrän strax innan de gav sig ut.

■ LÄRDE SVENSKA

Svenska har de lärt sig snabbt och talar numera tydligt och väl vart modermål, om än med amerikanskt uttal. Men de hade inte gärna kunnat få lära sig grekiska, portugiska, »panska eller något annat av de »prak som används i de länder, dit mormonerna kan komma med sin mission.

Med 500 kronor i månaden klarar en kyrka. De träffar församlingsmedlemmar och andra missionärer.

■ STÄNGER DÖRREN

Men fem dagar i veckan missionerar de, träffar folk på gator och vägar, ringer på dörrar och söker presentera sin kyrkas familjeprogram, berättar om "Mormons bok".

— Visst stänger många dörren för oss. Vi blir kanske lite ledsna, men vi ger inte upp.

»sas hjälp kommer de både till Svalöv och Röstånga under sina turer.

De unga missionärernas dag är noga inrutad. Varje morgon reser de sig kl 6.30 från sängarna i rummet de hyr på Artillerigatan i Landskrona. Efter frukost följer halvannan timmes studier, särskilt i svenska språket, innan de är beredda att bege sig ut för att träffa människor. De nöjer sig med mat två gånger om dagen. Senast 22.30 meddelar deras schema att de ska sova.

Och det gör de! De två följer benhårt de regler som är uppsatta för dem.

»Vi arbetar hela tiden för var jänt inte på bio, röker inte, dricker inte (inte ens kaffe!).

■ ALLTID KAVAJ

Mandagarna har de för sig själva. De städar och ser över sina kläder 'alltid strikt utseende! Gar inte ut till soffunnan utan kavaj ens...) De skriver brev hem, rapporterar till distrikts-, zon- och Sverigeledare. Den senare bor i Stockholm och ansvarar för de unga missionärernas hälsa och välstånd. Till honom kan de alltid ringa om de behöver råd och stöd.

Om söndagarna cyklar de till Helsingborg, där mormönerna har en kyrka. De träffar församlingsmedlemmar och andra missionärer.

Både förklarar, att de aldrig blivit handgripligen utkastade, men vit de ändå märkt fientlighet i vissa lager. — Det finns de som trött oss »ara CIA-agenter» och fragat efter revolvern, berättar Russon förläget.

— Vi vet att kyrkan har någonting för oss alla, men vi försöker

Moderna missionärer, unga amerikaner, på väg till församlingsmedlem i Röstånga. Robert Russon och Marc Garrison avverkar många mil per cykel under ett par år i Sverige.

inte tvinga människor att lyssna till oss.

■ TANDLÄKARE

Marc Garrison avbröt en utbildning till tandläkare, då han gav sig på sin tvåariga missionstjänst i Sverige. När han återvänder om något år, ska han fortsätta stud rande fem år i tandläkarutbildningen.

Robert Russon är naturmänniska. Efter Sverige återvänder han hem för att ägna sig at viltvård.

Och bada förklarar de:

— Vi är mycket förtjusta i Sverige!

Det började med en uppenbarelse...

LANDSKRONA: Mormonerna, d v s Jesu Kristi kyrka av Sista Dagars Heliga, uppstod 1820 i nordöstra USA med ett en 14-årig yngling, Joseph Smith, fick en uppenbarelse. Enligt denna kunde han leta rätt på en urkund, graverad på metallplåtar, som innehöll det folks religiösa och världsliga historia, som var den röda mannens förfäder och daterade sig fram omkring 600 f Kr till 421 e Kr.

Han översatte urkunden, som nu

är känd som "Mormons bok" och som brukas tillsammans med bibeln.

Kyrkan började organiseras 1830 och växte till under ständig förföljelse från villkanande. Redan 1837 började missionsverksamheten i England och senare i bl a Sverige. Samtidigt drog mormonerna västerut från sina första uppehallsplatser i nordöstra USA. Till slut kom man till dalen vid Stora Saltsjön, där Salt Lake City, mor-

monernas huvudstad, grundades.

För närvarande finns över 4 miljoner mormoner i över 7.000 församlingar i hela världen. Mormonerna ägnar sig at i första hand familjen och kyrkan. Mormonerna true på ett liv i evighet och att familjerna efter döden åter formas i himlen. Numera ägnar sig dock inte mormoner al mangilfte, vilket de varit kända för i tidigare sammanhang.

Många svenska släktforskare har

kommit i kontakt med de mikrofilmade svenska kyrkoböckerna. Denna filming har utförts just genom mormonernas försorg. En kopia av alla svenska kyrkböcker finns i ett bergrum i närheten av Salt Lake City. Här kan man forska reda på sina förfader. Man ska bli var träffas efter den jordiska döden!

På det sättet har svensk släktforskning fått glädje av mormonernas tro.

Här håller de tva mormon-missionärerna på hos Sören Bergsman i Åsmundtorp.

Mormoner i Karlskoga:
— Vi offrar allt för vår kyrka

— Vi offrar allt för vår kyrka. Herren har befallt oss att sprida budskapet över hela världen. Vi har sanningen om livet...
Amerikanerna Marc Garrisson och Russel Kemp missionerar i Sverige och just nu i Karlskoga. De är utsända av Jesu Kristi Kyrka av Sista Dagars Heliga. De är vad som populärt kallas mormoner och här för att värva nya själar för sin tro.

Mormonkyrkan har ca 150 unga missionärer verksamma i Sverige och 23 000 över hela världen. Alla är omkring 20 år gamla.

Marc Garrisson har haft Karlskoga som arbetsfält i tre månader och i dagarna kom Russel Kemp hit, också han utvald för mormonernas mission i Sverige.

Marc talar bra svenska efter tio månader i Sverige. Han berättar att de efter studier och prov ansetts värdiga att bege sig ut i världen. De stannar i Sverige under två år och skiftar uppehållsplats enligt order från kyrkans ledning i Stockholm.

De här amerikanska ungdomarna gör stora uppoffringar för att kunna komma ut i världen och missionera. De har ingen lön från mormonkyrkan utan får ta egna sparade medel. Familjerna ställer också upp med pengar. De utsända mormonerna måste leva under mycket knappa omständigheter.

— Bryr oss inte om flickor

— Vi arbetar hela tiden för vår kyrka. Bryr oss inte om flickor. Går inte på bio. Röker och dricker inte. Ja, vi dricker inte ens kaffe eller te för det är inte nyttigt för kroppen, säger Marc Garrisson och tillägger att en mormon dock får dansa...

De värvar själar i Karlskoga. Mormonerna Marc Garrisson och Russel Kemp. — Vi offrar allt för vår kyrka. Herren har befallt oss att sprida budskapet över hela världen, säger de båda.
Foto: STEN NÖJD

Mormonerna tror på att Kristus ska återkomma och man tror på levande profeter. Det var Joseph Smith som startade mormonkyrkan — d v s Jesu Kristi Kyrka av Sista Dagars Heliga — år 1820 då han som 14-åring fick en uppenbarelse. Kyrkan började organiseras tio år senare och växte sen under ständig förföljelse från oliktänkande. Till Sverige kom de första "missionärerna" i mitten av förra seklet. Här har man idag ca 6 000 medlemmar och i hela världen ca 4 miljoner.

Mormonerna ägnar sig i första hand åt familjen och kyrkan. Man tror på ett evigt liv och att familjerna efter döden återförenas i himlen. Mormonerna påbjöd förr mångagifte.

Marc och Russel har en noga iinrutad arbetsdag. Varje morgon står man upp klockan halv sju på rummet man hyr i Karlskoga. Efter frokust följer någon timmas studier, särskilt i svenska språket, innan de är beredda att ge sig ut för att träffa människor. Alltid uppträder de strikt i kavaj och slips. De förkunnar sitt budskap på gator och de ringer på hos folk. De undervisar också i skolorna. Senast klockan elva på kvällen ska de gå till sängs enligt schemat.

Många stänger dörren

Marc Garrisson:
— Visst stänger många dörren för oss. En del skäller ut oss. Vi blir-förstås ledsna, men ger inte upp. Vi försöker dock inte tvinga oss på människor. Här i Karlskoga tycker jag människorna för det mesta är vänliga. De flesta ger sig tid att lyssna på vad vi har att säga.

Efter de två missionsåren i Sverige återvänder de båda till USA för att skaffa sig en utbildning. Marc tänker bli tandläkare och Russel försäkringsman.
TORBJÖRN ANDERSON

77

Missionärer i Stenungsund lever på 600 kr i månaden

STENUNGSUND (Bohuslä-ningen) De lever på c:a 600 kronor i månaden. Arbetar ungefär 60 timmar i veckan. En stor del av den tiden anslås till studier i svenska.

Mormonerna, eller, som rörelsens anhängare officiellt heter "Jesu Kristi Kyrka av Sista dagars heliga" – ett "ödesmättat" namn gör onekligen stora personliga uppoffringar. Det förstår man efter ett samtal med fyra missionärer från rörelsen ifråga: stockholmaren Sören Lindqvist och John Cracroft från Salt Lake City i Utah, mormonernas huvudort i USA.

De två verkar nu några månader i Stenungsund. För tillfället hade de besök av två missionärer, verksamma i Angered i Göteborg, Marc Stephen Garrisson och Phillip Robert Hurlbert, också de amerikanare.

UTOMLANDS

En grundläggande del av mormonernas religionsutövning är just att sprida sin tro till hela världens folk. Alla rättrogna – främst då männen – vill offra två år av sitt liv till missionsverksamhet i något land utanför USA. Många gör det också. De här fyra är bara en liten del av alla de ynglingar som lämnar studier, arbete, hem och familj för att på egen bekostnad resa och bo utomlands under två år.

600 kronor att leva på i vårt dyra Sverige. Hur kan det gå?
– Vi måste naturligtvis pruta av på all komfort. Vi två bor ihop, hyran tar ända hälften av kostnaderna, berättar Sören. Så hushållar vi för oss själva och delar på matutgifterna. Det reducerar ju kostnaderna men det är klart att några utsvävningar i matväg räcker det absolut inte till. Vi röker inte, dricker inte kaffe eller te. Det hör till våra absoluta regler att avhålla oss från allt, som vi vet innehåller gift av något slag. Givetvis räcker inte heller pengarna till "kläder eller några förströelser, som kostar pengar.

Fyra mormonmissionärer på "turné" pr cykel i Stenungsund: "Äldsten" Sören Lindqvist, äldsten John Cracroft, Marc Stephen Garrisson och Philips Robert Hurlbert jr.

Det krävs hängivelse för saken för att frivilligt avstå från all komfort. Därtill kommer ju åtskilliga praktiska svårigheter in i bilden för att kunna bo och verka i ett främmande land, många ganger långt hemifrån och med ett kulturmönster och språk så olikt ens eget. – Ja, vi måste läga ned stor del av vår tid på att lära oss så mycket av det främmande språket som möjligt, bekräftar amerikanarna.

Vad är det då mormonmissionärerna vill na med sitt trappnötande, sina möten, sin uppsökande verksamhet på gator och torg?
– Vi vill dela med oss av vårt budskap. Vittna om att Jesu Kristi Kyrka är återupprättad på jorden. Det vet vi genom var profet och ledare Joseph Smith. Han har fått den uppenbarelsen och auktoritet att sprida den genom Gud själv, säger Sören.

OVETANDE

Vi svenskar i gemen vet väldigt lite om vad "Sista Dagars Heliga" egentligen är för religion. För

oss är en mormon en person som lever i månggifte. – Det stämmer inte idag, säger Sören. Från början förekom det av praktiska skäl. "Mormonerna" – lat oss kalla dem det för enkelhetens skull även om det inte är fullt korrekt – var förr utsatta för stor förföljelse. Många män led martyrdöden och ett stort kvinnöverskott blev följden. Eftersom vår religion värnar om familjebanden och äktenskap räknas som något man bör sträva efter så var månggifte en praktisk lösning. Idag följer vi naturligtvis vårt lands kulturmönster och lever i engifte.

På tal om äktenskap och familj är det värt att påpeka att mormonerna alltså lägger mycket stor vikt vid familjesammanhållning. Minst en gang i veckan samlas hela familjen för att ägna sig enbart åt varandra. Familjefadern leder en andakt men man kan också syssla med mera "världsliga" ting. Man diskuterar, man kanske spelar något sällskapsspel, man sysslar med något ting

som alla kan deltaga i gemensamt.

Huvudsaken är att stunden främjar sammanhållningen, skyddar familjen från att splittras i olika intressen, berättar de fyra.

KRISTNA?

En fråga som en mormon i Sverige ofta får är: Är ni kristna? På det blir svaret ett absolut ja. Protestanter: nej. De sista dagars heliga gör inte, som de själva säger, anspråk på någon succession fran nagon annan kyrka eller sekt. – Vi är en religion "för oss själva" men en kristen tro, säger Sören. Det kan låta motsägelsefullt men motiveras av att mormonerna tror på Kristus och den heliga treenigheten. Bibeln intar ofta platsen bredvid "Mormons bok" i deras bokhylla. Vad som skiljer protestanten och katoliken från mormonen. För att försöka förklara det kort: mormonerna har sina profeter, av vilka grundaren Joseph Smith var den förste, som man erkänner som direkta medier fran Gud.

Here are some ideas to keep in mind while contacting nonmembers.

• It is important to develop and use creative approaches. Don't use only one or two approaches in every situation. Tailor the approach to meet the needs of the person you're talking to. Look for clues that might help you know what part of the gospel might interest them.

• "Use boldness, but not overbearance." (Alma 38:12.) Don't be apologetic *or* pushy. This is a tough balance to strike, but you can do it.

• Be sensitive to other commitments and responsibilities the nonmember might have.

• Love the people. Have an attitude of service and a desire to bless the lives of others. If others see how you really do care about their eternal welfare, they are much more likely to listen.

• Esteem all people as yourself, and don't be condescending. That is, don't feel and act like you are lowering yourself to talk to nonmembers about the truth that you have. Instead, be respectful to all people.

• Make a return appointment. Your goal is to schedule a time to visit with the whole family at home. Let investigators know what to expect during the visit. You might want to mention such items as length of visit, content, and desired number of visits.

• Have a friendly attitude. Leave every contact as a friend — whether he accepts your message or not. Missionaries are ambassadors of peace and goodwill. People with no initial interest may later seek more information because of a missionary's friendly attitude.

Brigham Young, our second prophet, gives a very good example of how we should tailor our message to the receiver.

Whether it is a credit to me or not, that is with the Lord, but he has given me the ability that whenever I have wished to receive favors from those who knew me not, I have obtained them. I know it is the custom of many elders to say, "I am a 'Mormon' elder; will you keep me overnight?" and he is at once spurned from the doors of the stranger. Whether it is credit to me or not, I never told them I was a "Mormon" elder until I got what I wanted. I have thus stopped at many a house and had the privilege of introducing the principles of our religion, and they have exclaimed, "Well, if this is Mormonism, my house shall be your home as long as you stay in this neighborhood," when, perhaps if I had said, "I am a 'Mormon' elder at the first they would have refused me their hospitality. I can say to the world they used me pretty well, and I have no fault to find with them in this respect. I have been abused sometimes by priests, but on such occasion I have ever been ready to defend the cause of righteousness and preach the gospel to all. (Brigham Young, *Journal of Discourses,* 12:171)

Remember the courage we talked about earlier? Well, right now is your first chance to try it out. Think back to the suggestions you can give to members for ways to share the gospel. Then pick one or two methods and prayerfully decide on a friend or relative or acquaintance with whom you will share the gospel. Then go approach them about the gospel.

Does this assignment scare you? It does?! Good! Now you know how members will feel when you ask them to discuss the gospel with their friends. And it will be much easier to convince timid members that sharing the gospel is fun and reasonably painless if you can truthfully say, "I felt the same way. But then I learned how much fun it is."

In all seriousness, there is no time like the present to overcome your inhibitions about sharing the gospel. And like jumping off the high dive into the pool, the toughest part is the first step. And once you have found someone close to you who is ready to listen to the gospel then you can get welcome help from the missionaries.

So go ahead and do this assignment. Nothing can beat the experience that awaits you. Once you have an appointment with the missionaries then come back. There is still more we need to discuss about your preparation.

Good, you're back!

Now that you know how to introduce a friend or relative to the gospel, review the basic pattern for success. First you must make a list of all of your non-member friends and acquaintances. Then after prayerfully considering each person and their circumstances select your three most likely candidates. Then decide who of the three is most ready to accept the gospel. After you have made your decision, present it to the Lord. Ask for His approval. You should have felt His influence all along, but He still wants you to make the decision first. He will answer you. Then go ahead and repeat the process as you decide how to approach your friend about the gospel.

One important note: it is inevitable that you will spend more time with your friend as he or she listens to the gospel message. Should your friend elect not to accept the gospel it is still important that you maintain your friendship. Please continue to show the same love and interest in your friend before, during, and after the discussions, whether the whole process ends in baptism or not. After all, the person is still your friend, whether or not he joins the Church. If he elects not to investigate further, so be it. That does not mean he has rejected you as a friend or that he will never be converted to the gospel.

I know that approaching people about the gospel is difficult (I've been doing it for years). But I also know that if you will gulp down your fears and forge ahead, you will be filled with the Spirit. Continue to attack your fears and soon you will begin each day with a feeling of expectation and excitement. You will have discovered the fun of missionary work.

On a recent business trip to San Antonio, Texas, I was upgraded from coach to first class by some inspired gate agent who knew that I needed to sit next to the young man who was sitting in seat 2D. As I sat down, the last thing on my mind was a chat about the gospel. I had just gotten my own copy of the new discussions and the pamphlets that you hand out to your investigators. I said "Hi," to this young man, put my briefcase down under the seat in front of me and began to read. I couldn't help noticing him rubbernecking the discussions. I asked him if he knew anything about the Church. He told me, very matter of factly, that he was half Mormon. Since I had never met a half Mormon before, I couldn't help laughing and inquiring what he meant by that. He said that his best friend was just getting ready to go on a mission himself and that he really respected the LDS Church for its beliefs and moral ethics.

Our discussion went on for the rest of the flight and ranged from what he knew about the church to how he could get a testimony himself. It concluded by my giving him my entire newly obtained pamphlets which accompany the discussions. I encouraged him to read then pray about what he had heard about the Church and to encourage his friend to participate in the missionary discussions with him. I also told him that he would make a great missionary.

I have the utmost confidence that anyone with the love of Christ and his Church has the ability to approach people about the gospel and to work with members in finding people to teach. Quite often the members prove to be the most difficult, but with some prayer and dedication to your gospel message you will win.

Challenge

- Please do the following:
- Read the pamphlet *I Need a Friend.*
- Read "Coordination with the Branch or Ward" and "Finding People to Teach,," in the *Missionary Handbook*, pp. 30-32.
- Personally contact a friend about the Church and submit a referral.
- Work with your local full-time missionaries for an evening.

Chapter 5

Teaching

Love is the only bow on life's dark
cloud. It is the Morning and Evening Star.
It shines upon the cradle of the babe,
and sheds its radiance upon the quiet tomb.
It is the Mother of Art, inspirer of poet,
patriot, and philosopher. It is the air and
light of every heart, builder of every home,
kindler of every fire on every hearth. It
was the first dream of immortality. It fills
the world with melody . . . . Love is the magician,
the enchanter, that changes worthless things to
joy, and makes right royal kings of common clay.

Robert G. Ingersoll

Scriptures:
Matthew 28:19, D & C 42:14, D & C 50:14, Jacob 1:19, Jacob 2:2

Elder Scott, Argentina Mission

> *When I got my mission call to Argentina, about the only thing I knew about the country was that it was a South American nation filled with a history of political violence and a rich gaucho heritage. Later I discovered that my call was to the same mission where an elder from my stake had been kidnapped by desperados and was mistakenly shot and left for dead by the police. Nevertheless, I was excited about the call and knew that the Lord would protect me.*

After a short time at home to buy missionary clothes and a couple of months in the MTC, I found myself stepping off the plane in Rosario. The small international airport was filled with federal police armed with machine guns. I was greeted by the elders from the mission home and driven to our hotel.

The next day I was assigned to begin my mission in Firmosa, a smaller city in northern Argentina, just across the river from Paraguay. On the way I met my senior companion, and we traveled the rest of the long 14-hour trip together.

Over the next few weeks I really learned to love the Argentine people. I really missed my family and home but knew I was doing what I should. One Sunday we were walking home from church and we passed the local Federal Police Headquarters. One of the rifle-bearing guards called us over to the station. Knowing we had done nothing wrong, we respectfully followed his orders. They made me wait in the lobby while they took my companion down a hallway. I didn't really know what to do other than trust in the Lord and wait for them to bring him back. They finger printed us, took mug shots and recorded all of our vital information then let us go. After we were a few blocks away, I asked my companion what they had done with him. He recounted that they had taken him and told him that if we weren't careful they would kill us. Confused by this interesting confrontation, we made it a habit to avoid the Policia Federal as much as possible.

Things went fine for a few weeks, then the Argentine military seized the Falkland Islands (Islas Malvinas) which are also claimed by England. A war broke out between the two countries. The mission president confined all missionaries to our apartments because no one was sure how the people would react towards us since we were foreigners from the U.S. The Policia Federal immediately came to our apartment and questioned us to find out just what we were doing in Argentina and get our personal information again. One of them seemed quite friendly and wanted to come back to talk to us about the U.S. As a policy we tried to avoid people who were only interested in the United States, but since we could not leave our apartment to talk to anyone we thought we might as well make the best of his inquisitiveness and told him to come back anytime and we would be there. He said that he would have special permission from his superiors to come see us.

Sure enough, about a week later, the same man came back to our apartment. We weren't too excited about it but at least it was a break from studying which was all we could really do. The man was very respectful and unpretentious. He took off his gun, told us that his name was Alberto Galeano and that he was not really there to hear about the U.S. but that he wanted us to teach him the gospel of Jesus Christ. When he said that, my lower jaw nearly hit the floor. We immediately grabbed our flip charts and scriptures and started the discussions. He was the most humble and honest man I taught my whole mission. He accepted all that we taught. We taught him how to pray and asked him if he would like to offer a prayer. We knelt and he offered one of the most sincere prayers I have ever heard. He told us that he wanted to find some way to come to the United States to be baptized because he knew that he would lose his job and be badly persecuted if anyone there found out about it.

We taught him nearly every night for the two weeks we were restricted to our apartment and each of his visits were anxiously awaited.

As always happens in the mission field, I was soon transferred. I was so busy in my other areas that I couldn't keep in touch with him as I would have liked to, but a few months later I got a letter from him and tears came to my eyes as I read that he and his family had secretly been baptized.

I learned many things from my experience with this great man. I was able to see just how much the Lord blesses and protects those who are found in his service — even in times of danger. Alberto was a great inspiration to me for the remainder of my mission and will be throughout my life.

•　　•　　•

Missionaries are sent forth "to teach the children of men the things which I [the Lord] have put into your hands by the power of my Spirit." (D&C 43:15.) You are called and set apart to teach the restored gospel of Jesus Christ.

This message has three basic truths:

1. *The Divine Sonship of Christ.* He stands at the head of our His church. (See Mosiah 5:8; D & C 18:23-25.)

2. *The Mission of Joseph Smith.* (See D & C 1:17; 5:10; 136:36-40.)

3. *The Divinity of The Church of Jesus Christ of Latter-day Saints.*

These and other supporting truths are contained in the missionary discussions. It is not only important that you memorize the discussions, but that you also understand them fully.

As you gain experience in teaching the gospel discussions, you will gain an appreciation for the organization and content of the discussions. Each word of the missionary discussions is carefully reviewed by numerous members of the Church. Each phrase, example, supporting scripture, and question is prayerfully selected by members of a Church committee. The members of this committee have spent hundreds, even thousands of hours probing, praying, pondering the content of these discussions. Only when they are certain the material is clear, accurate, and absolutely essential can it be included in the proselyting discussions. While the missionary discussions are brief, you will find that if you study them completely (giving attention to questions, supporting truths, and other suggestions) that the discussions are really quite comprehensive. Of course, they are just the basics of the gospel, but these basics are essential for investigators to understand the gospel and the commitment that it requires.

A story is told about a preacher and an actor. "How is it," demanded the preacher of the great actor, "that I, in teaching divine doctrines, produce so little effect upon my congregation, while you can so easily rouse the passions of your listeners by speaking fiction?"

"Because," responded the actor, "I recite falsehoods as if they were true, while you deliver truths as if they were fiction." The lesson of this story is true. You need to not only understand and to have a testimony of the basic truths which the lessons teach, but you need to have a personal commitment and an excitement which match the message which you are giving.

Occasionally, you will need to alter the order in which the discussions or various concepts are taught. You may also spend much more time teaching the word of wisdom or some other precept that is difficult for a particular investigator to comprehend or accept. But in general, please, follow the prescribed methods of teaching the discussions. And please teach the discussions. The doctrines of temple marriage, the law of consecration, and other teachings may be interesting, but they are not necessary for conversion and hence need not be taught by you. Your investigators will have numerous chances to learn about many other aspects of the gospel as they study, pray, and attend meetings on Sunday.

You will frequently be asked about your political, economic or social views. This is particularly true if you are serving in a foreign country. It is best to tactfully decline to discuss such topics with investigators. For one thing, your mission is to declare the gospel, not discuss political theory. And for another, your political and social views, no matter how insightful, will often be viewed as representing the official stand of the Church. Discussions of this type can offer you nothing. Avoid them at all costs.

By now you are ready to tackle the missionary discussions. You have already read the discussions several times and have practiced teaching them with a friend or family member. While it may not be possible to memorize the missionary discussions completely before you leave on your mission, begin now to learn them by memorizing the first concept in the first discussion *The Plan of our Heavenly Father*. Unless you already have your call, you should learn (or at least become familiar with) the discussions in your native tongue. Even if you are called to a foreign mission, understanding the discussions' content will help you learn them much more quickly in a foreign language.

By now you have done much that will prepare you for the challenge of teaching the gospel. With this preparation you are now in a much better position to take advantage of the program in the missionary training center. There you can expand and refine your teaching skills and give fuller attention to learning a language if necessary. Your time there, as with your time in the mission field will go much smoother and bring greater rewards depending on how you act now — on how well you prepare.

You will find that the discussions go hand in hand with the scriptures. All that you say should motivate your investigators to study and ponder the scriptures. Your own understanding of the scriptures will govern, in part, your ability to teach effectively.

How are you doing with your scripture study? Have you been reading the scriptures on a daily basis, especially the Book of Mormon?

If you have, then great! What have you learned? How much have you grown? What rewards has this preparation brought you? What questions do you have? If you have not kept up with the challenge, start right now. Yes, now. Put a bookmark in this spot and go grab your Book of Mormon. Open up to Alma, Chapter 26. Read it. Then come back and we will have a short quiz.

Back already? Great. Here are a few questions:

1. Why is Ammon so overjoyed?
2. Among what people did he and his brethren preach the gospel?
3. What kind of hardships did they suffer?
4. Were they successful?
5. About whom is Ammon boasting?
6. Can you list at least two personal attributes that the missionaries possessed which helped them succeed.

How did you do on the quiz? Did you learn something while you read? Did you feel the Spirit as you pondered each question? You might try this very same exercise with your investigators. If they read the assignments you have given them, have them review what they read. Offer to answer any questions they might have. If they have not read what you asked them to read, then stop right now and read it with them. Then ask them to review what they have just read, and answer any of their questions.

You can see how important reading the scriptures, and following through on assignments is to feeling the Spirit.

Teaching With The Spirit and With Love

The Lord not only tells missionaries *what* to teach, but he also tells them *how* they should teach. There are two important guiding principles. The first is to *teach by the spirit* — to live and teach in such a way that the Holy Ghost can bear witness of your message and guide you in what you say.

Please read the following scriptures: D & C 42:12-14, D & C 50:17-22, D & C 100:5-6, 2 Nephi 33:1

Remember that although you are the messenger, it is the Holy Ghost who converts. You must teach under His influence if you are to be understood.

Elder Robert L. Simpson tells this story about a missionary who taught by the power of the Holy Ghost.

A young man . . . was called into the mission field. He felt inadequate for the call — his grammar was poor, he did not know how to talk to people, and he felt that he could not carry out his mission. The reason he had this inferiority complex was because he had to quit school when he was fifteen years of age because his father had passed away. This boy became the family breadwinner — he had to take over the ranch in Wyoming. The bishop assured him, however, that his place was in the mission field now that he was nineteen.

So into the mission field he traveled, half-way around the world, and there on his very first day he was told that Sister Johnson was having the missionaries for dinner, which was the custom of that mission. On the first day they went to her home and tasted the food of that land and learned something of the customs. Sister Johnson's husband was not a member of the Church. He knew the scriptures very, very well — he knew everything that a Mormon missionary did not know on his first day in the mission field. After dinner he would get these missionaries in a corner. He would try to embarrass them, and he found great delight in doing so. More often than not the missionaries went home determined that was not going to happen to them again, so they set their alarm clocks up thirty minutes earlier in order that they might get some extra studying in.

But here comes our young cowboy from Wyoming, feeling inadequate in his calling. Mr. Johnson was in the corner with him after dinner, and the missionary was embarrassed till tears came to his eyes. The thought came into his heart, 'I will go to my mission president in the morning and tell him that I must be released. I have come into the mission field unprepared.' Just then something lifted him right out of his chair, and he stood up to his full six-foot-four-inches of Wyoming cowboy. He reached over and took Mr. Johnson by the shoulders, and he pulled him real close. He said, 'Now, Mr. Johnson, I do not know how to argue these things with you. I do not know how to debate with you. I have not had a lot of schooling, but I know why I have to come half-way around the world. If you will just stand here for four or five minutes, I am going to tell you about it.' Mr. Johnson had no choice. The young elder from Wyoming then had a captive audience. Then, for the next five or six minutes, this young cowboy from Wyoming told the man the Joseph Smith story — the story that rang true in his heart. He had been taught the story at the knee of his mother. He used to read the story as he rode the range. He loved it and he knew that it was true, and so he told it to Mr. Johnson with all of the sincerity of his heart. After five or six minutes had gone by, there were tears in other eyes.

To make a long story short, there was a baptism about four or five weeks later. I think you know who was baptized and who did the baptizing. Mr. Johnson had heard the Joseph Smith story from every missionary who had ever been in his home — some who had been all the way through college, some who had their gifts developed; but never had he heard it with the gift of the Spirit of God *like he heard it from the unschooled lips of a cowboy from Wyoming on that wonderful day. He was listening to something from the heart of this young missionary into his heart--bearing witness to him, 'This young man is telling me the truth. Poorly as he is telling it, poor as his grammar is, I know that it is true because God is revealing it to me.' And he joined this great church."* (Robert L. Simpson,"Gifts of the Spirit", *Speeches of the Year,* 1966, pp. 9-11.)

Brigham Young says that nothing short of teaching by the power of the Holy Ghost will do.

I had only travelled a short time to testify to the people, before I learned this one fact, that you might prove doctrine from the Bible till doomsday, and it would merely convince a people, but would not convert them. You might read the Bible from Genesis to Revelations, and prove every iota that you advance, and that alone would have no converting influence upon the people. Nothing short of a testimony by the power of the Holy Ghost would bring light and knowledge to them — bring them in their hearts to repentance. Nothing short of that would ever do. (Brigham Young ,*Journal of Discourses,* 5:327.)

A missionary, on returning from his mission, was asked how many people he converted. "Only two," he said, "and they soon went inactive."

The questioner was about to give his condolences when the missionary continued. "But the Lord converted many. And today they're stronger in the Church than ever." As you serve your mission you will soon realize that you are a tool in the Lord's hand. It is your faith and testimony that gets you up out of bed when you are dog tired, that helps you learn a language and the discussions when your head feels like it's ready to bust open, that helps give you the courage to commit someone to baptism or that helps you accept the rejection of the gospel from someone you have grown to love. And it is the Lord that will bless you richly for your labors.

It is time for me to ask a question that I asked you earlier on. Why are you going on a mission? As you sift the various reasons in your mind, I want you to ask yourself: "What role did the Holy Ghost play in my decision to serve a mission?" Once you get beyond duty, the wishes of parents or friends, tradition, and any other reasons that might have influenced you, I think you will discover that in the end it was the Holy Ghost who convinced you to serve a mission. That same influence is necessary for converting people to the gospel. You will quickly discover that teaching without the influence of the Spirit yields nothing. Neither you nor your investigators will be edified. On the other hand, as you preach and teach the gospel under the direction of the Spirit you will feel consistently uplifted and your investigators will know what you teach is true.

There are times when the Spirit is not present during a discussion. If so, try to analyze in your mind what seems to be hampering the influence of the Spirit. Sometimes there are so many distractions in a home that your investigators will have little opportunity to ponder the truths of your message. Hence, they cannot feel the Spirit. Sometimes the people you teach are contentious, and the Spirit leaves. Sometimes food or drink is served during the discussion, which detracts from the Spirit. Perhaps you and your companion made the mistake of quarreling before you arrived to teach the discussion and the Holy Ghost refuses to be present. Or perhaps you have not prepared as you ought. The list goes on.

In any case if the Spirit is not present, and you feel after evaluating the situation that He will not come, then terminate the discussion and try to reschedule another. If possible, try to correct whatever is detracting from the Holy Ghost's influence.

Sometimes all it takes is for you to have your investigator turn off the television or simply to offer an additional word or prayer. But remember, it is the Holy Ghost that converts. You, as a well-prepared laborer, can become partners with Him in bringing people the blessings of the gospel. But without His influence you are merely discussing ideologies.

To qualify for the constant companionship of the Holy Ghost, you must remain constantly worthy by guarding your thoughts and actions and obeying mission rules. You must also remain constantly prepared by reviewing the discussions, praying and studying the scriptures by yourself and with your companion, practicing proselyting techniques, planning and setting goals, and by studying the language (where applicable). Remember, as you keep the commandments of the Lord (including mission rules) you are entitled to the companionship and influence of the Spirit. His presence will bring you success and joy in your labors.

In addition to the power of the Spirit, there is another power which can wield great influence. It is called love.

Please read the following scriptures: 1 Corinthians 1:1 and Moroni 7:45-47.

Both Moroni and Paul have told us that charity, or the pure love of Christ is our highest human achievement and if we are possessed of it then our works done in love will last and at the last day it will be well with us.

Nothing is so much calculated to lead people to forsake sin as to take them by the hand, and watch over them with tenderness. When persons manifest the least kindness and love to me, O what power it has over my mind, while the opposite course has a tendency to harrow up all the harsh feelings and depress the human mind. (Joseph Smith, *History of the Church*, 5:23-24.)

Time and time again in this book, I have stressed the importance of loving the people you are called to serve and of showing respect for their culture, their laws, and their beliefs. It is doubly important that when you teach, you do so with a true spirit of love. Never condescend to those you teach. The reason is obvious. Can you really love someone you look down on? And can you adequately teach someone the gospel when you are not truly concerned for their welfare?

Read the following examples showing missionaries teaching by the Spirit, teaching with love, or teaching without these guiding principles. After reading each example, ask yourself whether that incident is an example of teaching with love.

• Elder Howard and Elder Dean are teaching the Jones family. Tonight they had planned to teach about the word of Wisdom. But during the discussion Elder Howard felt impressed to talk to them about baptism. So he taught the Baptismal challenge.

• "Now here is a scripture from your own Bible that proves what you just said is wrong!"

• "We certainly don't want to force you to do anything against your will, but would you mind sharing with us your feelings about why you don't want to come to church?"

• Elder Hall is teaching the lesson about the Savior. He notices a warm, wonderful feeling in the meeting. He pauses and says, "Can you feel that wonderful feeling?" The family acknowledges that they can. "That is the Holy Ghost bearing witness to the truthfulness of our message," Elder Hall adds.

• Elder Harris has been asleep during most of the meeting, but after a nudge from his companion, he wakes up to bear his testimony. There is an awkward feeling in the room and Elder Harris is slightly embarrassed. However, he states that he has felt the Spirit in the meeting and he knows that what his companion says is true.

• "Mr. Brown, if I understand correctly, you say that you have given an honest effort, but you just can't seem to be able to give up smoking. Is that right? There is something we can do to help." Then they discuss fasting, prayer, the Lord's blessing, etc.

• Sister Morris and her companion were teaching Miss Thomas. During the second discussion, Miss Thomas asked, "Could you tell me, if I pray to God for help in getting a job, will he help me with something like that?" Sister Morris replied, "I don't see what that has to do with the lesson we're teaching!"

Teaching by the Spirit means listening to His whisperings as you teach. Often you will feel impressed to ask a certain question or to review a certain principle. There are times when you will feel you should bear your testimony. All of these instances are teaching by the Spirit. If you have prepared and seek His influence, you will always find it. I promise.

Teaching with love means simply to have empathy for those whom you teach and to possess a genuine interest in their welfare. If you love the people, you will never try to make them feel inferior, stupid, or unworthy. You will try to help them understand the gospel and will be understanding of their fears and reservations in accepting it. Through your testimony and love you will help them understand the gentleness and kindness of the Lord Jesus Christ and the tremendous love evident in His great plan.

I remember in one family that we taught the father was totally involved in some far out, metaphysical religion. He believed that he could see through people. He was kind of crazy. The mother was a little embarrassed because of the father. The kids thought their father was nuts, too. Missionaries had come to this family and got into a teaching situation, and they were always turned off, or made fun of the father. When my companion and I left after the first meeting with this family, we turned to each other and said, "What have the last missionaries here in this area left us?" We looked beyond that, though, and realized that this was a family. The father definitely had a problem, but there were also three sons. My companion looked at me and said, "What are those sons going to do if we don't introduce them into the church and really get them involved?" He said, "Why don't we just ignore the father, but be very friendly to him, and concentrate on the mother and the sons?" With that in mind, in weeks that family was baptized. The father is probably still off somewhere in space. He may yell at the missionaries, but they'll just smile and never yell back.

It was just a fun experience full of pure love. We weren't going just for numbers. What we saw was young boys who needed the church, and a mother who needed the support that she didn't receive from her husband. We also saw young boys going on missions themselves.

You can practice teaching by the Spirit right now as you work with the missionaries in teaching the gospel to the friend you introduced to the gospel. During the discussions seek for the gentle nudging of the Spirit. You may feel impressed to share a personal experience at an appropriate point, or you may feel inspired to ask for specific blessings in a prayer you are asked to offer. Or you may simply feel inspired to say nothing and allow the missionaries to teach as they are inspired.

You can practice teaching with love by showing empathy for all of those with whom you come in contact. Regardless of how you are treated, act towards others as if they were the Savior. As you practice this you will come to love others, even those who are unfriendly or difficult to love.

Teaching Skills

Your duty as a teacher of the gospel is to ensure that your investigator:

- Understands the gospel;

- Accepts it as true;

- And will *commit* to the gospel by repenting and living the commandments.

Consider these three points each time you teach a discussion.

First, you teach the gospel as outlined in the discussion.

Second, you assess your investigator's understanding of what you have taught.

Third, you answer your investigator's questions about what you have taught and help them overcome fears and misconceptions.

The discussions employ many specific teaching skills to help the missionary *teach, assess,* and *strengthen.* Among these skills are the following: present; show a picture; use a scripture; give an example; bear testimony; ask questions to assess understanding, acceptance, and commitment; ask follow-up questions; restate; confirm; explain; invite to pray; relate problems to the Book of Mormon; show empathy; and promise specific blessings.

Now, before your mission is a great time to give particular attention to the teaching skills. Now you can pay greater attention to each skill as you practice teaching the discussions with a friend. Your knowledge of these skills will prove invaluable later on.

As you continue to memorize the discussions pay close attention to how these skills are incorporated into each lesson. Perhaps you have noticed some already. For example, in *The Restoration* discussion, how can you help Mr. Brown comprehend the need for Christ to restore his church? In the discussion *The Plan of Salvation,* what example can you employ to illustrate how a body and a spirit are related to one another? In teaching the basic commandments, how can you assess Mr. Brown's understanding of the law of tithing?

As you memorize the discussions, pay particular attention to the supplemental material. If you do, you can help Mr. Brown understand the need for a restored church, the relationship of spirit to body, and his responsibility when asked to live the law of tithing.

Learn these skills now, and you will have the chance to refine them later in the Missionary Training Center. Ignore them for the moment, and you can learn them in the missionary training center and work on refining them in the field. As a smart prospective missionary, you will, I think, realize the advantages to beginning now.

Friendshipping

As I mentioned earlier, friendshipping is an important part of the conversion process. But friendshipping is important during each stage of your investigators' conversion. Friendshippers come from members of the Church who are willing to befriend and maintain contact with investigators. The friendshipper is ideally the same member who gave you the referral. If not, you can find someone from the local ward or branch to help you.

In previous chapters we discussed how tremendously effective members of the Church are in converting people to the Church. Among the reasons we listed were the members' empathy for investigators, their long-term relationship with investigators, their permanence in the local ward or branch, and the examples they have set. Every investigator should be friendshipped by a local member or family while receiving the discussions and beyond. These friendshippers can provide investigators with strength, stability, and empathy. The members can take the investigators to church meetings and activities and can invite them into their homes. The bottom line is that members get investigators involved in the day-to-day activities of members of the Church, exposing them to the church on very personal terms.

As mentioned earlier, your investigators should meet the bishop or branch president early on. It is important that they have contact with the people on whom they will lean for guidance and direction. Those investigators who are making committed progress towards baptism should also be assigned home teachers and visiting teachers. You should meet with your unit's mission leader and the quorum president to determine who will home teach your investigators. Although a formal "transition meeting" usually does not take place until after baptism, serious investigators should be introduced to these programs.

It is an absolute must that investigators attend church, preferably for several weeks, before being baptized. They desperately need exposure to the talks, the testimonies, the teachings in the gospel essentials class, and the lingering chatter after church. Your investigators should be comfortable at church before they enter the waters of baptism.

As suggested before, encourage your investigators to invite friends, neighbors, and relatives to listen to the gospel.

One method of teaching you should employ is group teaching. Teaching several investigators at once in small cottage meetings is an excellent way to present the gospel. Not only will you and your companion be using your time effectively, but you will reap all the benefits of group interaction. For one thing, investigators are more willing to listen to the gospel if they know others will be present (since they won't be the sole center of attention). For another, members of a group can often get each other excited and help each other be more honest about their reaction to your message. If one investigator has a question, you can bet that the others have similar concerns. Members of a group often encourage one another.

For example, they can give courage to one person who is afraid to pray publicly. Or they can share positive experiences they have had in following through on assignments you have given them. The key to being effective in group teaching is staying in control. You must direct the flow of discussion and keep it from straying.

Towards the end of my mission in Sweden I recorded on April 16, 1976, something which still haunts me to this day. My entry simply says,

Saw an old investigator today while on the train from Goteborg to Stockholm. We were really glad to see each other. Rudolph was a young man whom we had tracted out and taught several discussions to, but could never get him to catch the spirit or the need for the gospel. We talked for a while on the train about what we each had been doing. When I asked him if he was interested in hearing more about the Gospel, he said, 'Thanks, but not right now.'

My journal doesn't leave it at that. I was deeply affected by that meeting after all those months. I continued and wrote something which I have never forgotten in terms of the utter importance of our teaching people the gospel correctly with the Spirit. *"How's it going to feel on the other side if we taught them badly?"*

Challenge

Study "Fellowshipping," "Baptism," and "Confirmation," *Missionary Handbook,* pp. 32-39 and continue studying the discussions.

Chapter 6

Baptizing

Whether you think you can or
think you can't — you are right.

Henry Ford

Scriptures:
Joseph Smith History (PGP) 1:73, 1 Corinthians 3:7, D & C 42:14

Elder William
Australia, Melbourne Mission

*The two years I spent as a missionary in Australia were the
greatest two years of my life. I know that's a pretty worn-out cliche, but
I can't think of a better way to express my feelings about it. I learned
more about myself, the Church and other people during those two years
than I could have imagined possible.*

*I found that a big part of being a missionary is being able to
resolve people's concerns. This involves using the various missionary
tools to break down the walls of misconception, prejudice, apprehension
and ignorance that often lie between your testimony and the
investigator. Even the honest in heart cannot feel the Spirit of truth until
these barriers are cleared.*

Often, the hard part in resolving concerns is in determining exactly what the concerns are. I recall a time in my mission when I was transferred to an area that had not had missionaries in quite some time. Upon arriving in the area, my companion and I found a place to live and then went to visit the ward mission leader in hopes of obtaining any records the previous missionaries might have left. There was little in the records we found that we considered to be of any value, so we concentrated our efforts mainly on tracting and contacting members. There was one name in the old records, however, that my thoughts kept returning to. There was a man named Mike who the previous missionaries had apparently taught for quite awhile but never baptized. What interested me about this Mike was that he was deaf. Evidently, he was able to read lips very well, and that's how the missionaries were able to teach him. The records indicated that, though he seemed very receptive, he balked whenever baptism was mentioned. The missionaries worked with him for a couple of months before they finally gave up on him. Shortly thereafter, the missionaries were transferred and the area was closed. Mike had not been contacted since. What puzzled me was that the record did not indicate what Mike's objection or concern was. Why had he refused to be baptized?

We decided to pay a visit to Mike. The only address we had was a restaurant where he worked as a cook, so we showed up there one day. He immediately recognized us as missionaries and greeted us very enthusiastically. We talked with him for a few minutes and invited him over to our house for dinner later in the week. We realized that was kind of a strange thing to do, but it was the best idea we could come up with.

Hamburger was the limit of our combined culinary expertise, so that's what my companion and I prepared. Mike arrived, and we spent some time getting to know each other. The communication barrier was still a little bit of a problem, in spite of his exceptional lip-reading ability. My companion and I both felt the Spirit guiding us in the questions we asked as well as in our understanding of his answers. As we continued to discuss the Church and baptism, it suddenly became apparent what Mike's concern had been all along. Somewhere along the line, he developed the impression that all Mormons had to quit their jobs, dress up like missionaries and go around trying to convert people. When we questioned him about baptism, he replied, "But I have to work" and, "I don't have any suits."   The only Mormons that he had gotten to know very well were missionaries, and even when he attended church a couple of times, all the people he saw were dressed like the missionaries and talked about the same things.

All we had to do to resolve Mike's concerns was to explain to him that only a few of us were crazy enough to be missionaries and the rest were just normal people. We even took him down to a grocery store where a member of the Elder's Quorum presidency worked, so he could see that you could have a job and live a normal life and still be a Mormon. Mike was baptized the following weekend. He could have been baptized a year earlier, but someone had to find out what his concern was before it could be resolved.

•   •   •

Baptism and Fellowshipping

Generally, investigators are ready to be baptized when they have: accepted the gospel message; are attending Church; and are keeping the commandments. When they have thus progressed and are willing to become members of the Church, they will be interviewed by your district or zone leader to determine if they understand the gospel and the commitment they are making and to ensure that they are worthy to be baptized.

Special attention should be given to the baptism itself, ensuring that local leaders and members are present, that the tempo is reverent, but upbeat, and that the new converts' friends and family are made to feel welcome.

Once a person or family is baptized, the responsibility for their further progress shifts from the missionaries to the members. With the help of the local ward or branch mission leader, you should set up a transition meeting where the new converts can meet their home teachers. Gradually your contact with these new members will decrease, as they build new confidence and friendships in the local ward or branch.

It would be advantageous if friendshippers would continue as fellowshippers—possibly as home teachers—after the new converts have been baptized. This will give the converts a sense of continuity.

It is essential that other ward or branch members go out of their way to befriend the converts. The new members have given up many of their former friends and activities. They need new ones to take their place. If ever these new converts have needed a friend, now is the time.

Please read Moroni 6:4 and 2 Nephi 31:20.

New members of the Church need to be helped and strengthened as they grow in the gospel. They too must feel loved and welcome and they too must take on the responsibility to press forward with faith in Christ and to help their fellow saints.

President Thomas S. Monson tells this story about fellowshipping new members:

> *In a recent visit to the Italy, Rome Mission I noticed among the five hundred who were present that there were about twenty-four people, maybe thirty, who were wearing white carnations in their lapels. I said to President Larcher, 'What is the purpose of the white carnations?' He smiled and said: 'We have provided a white carnation for every person who has been baptized since our last district conference. They wear the white carnations so that all might know they are new members of God's kingdom, that we might fellowship them and make them welcome.' I watched those who wore the white carnations as they received handshake after handshake and embrace after embrace. Some were young; some were old. But those who wore the white carnation in the Italy, Rome*

*Mission were no more strangers or foreigners, but fellow citizens
with the saints, and of the household of God.' (Ephesians 2:19.)
They were being fellowshipped after having been converted and
baptized as members of God's kingdom. We can do likewise.*
(Thomas S. Monson, *"Motivating Missionaries,"* Address delivered
at the Seminar for New Mission Presidents, 23 June 1977, pp. 15-
16.)

Baptism isn't anything that you can "talk someone into." It isn't
something that can be proven mathematically or philosophically. Missionaries need to learn the steps of commitment that lead people to seek out the
Lord in humble prayer and to receive their own testimonies of the Gospel.
The first step is preparation. You must help build trust in those whom you
teach. You must help them recognize the spirit. You must help them
understand the gospel message and motivate them to gain testimonies of the
truth. In this preparation area you must be prepared to resolve any concerns
that they have. What if they are Jewish and cannot accept the idea of Christ.
Again, you will have to customize your teaching to resolve that concern.

The next step is to invite them to study, pray, be baptized, etc. It
takes courage for someone to commit to change their life. When you
challenge them to do this, be ready to resolve any concerns which they
might have.

Lastly, you need to follow up. Have the courage next time you meet
to see if they have done the things which they committed themselves to do.
If they haven't done them, don't jump on them and make them feel bad. Try
and understand the situation and resolve the concerns they have which
underlie their lack of follow through on their commitment. Conversion for
some is a quick, almost overnight process. For others it is a painful process
which takes months, even years. We need to love our investigators and be
patient with them and their mistakes just like our Heavenly Father is with
our own.

The purpose of missionary work is to help people know and follow
the Lord, to find greater happiness and peace in this life, and to inherit great

blessings in the life to come. The Lord will sustain you in your teaching efforts if you teach by the Spirit and with love. Fellowshipping by members helps investigators make the social transition into the Church. Of course, new converts have just begun their journey on the road to eternal life. Their future growth will require hardships, disappointments, and sacrifices. It will also bring love, peace, happiness, and hope. They will need the help of many friends along the way.

Challenge

Attend the next baptismal service that is held in your area. Imagine how it is going to feel when you are at a similar service with someone whom you have taught the gospel to.

Chapter 7

Keeping Going

Most people give up just when
they're about to achieve success. They
quit on the one yard line. They give up
at the last minute of the game one foot
from a winning touchdown.

H. Ross Perot

Scriptures:
D & C 127:4, D & C 66:12, D & C 106:8, Alma 38:10, D & C 61:9,
Alma Chapter 31, D & C 58:4, 1 Nephi 3:7, Deuteronomy 31:6, Alma 26:27,
D & C 121:1,2,7,9

Elder Rod
Gulfstates Mission

*One of the most discouraging times I had as a missionary was
trying to "sell" the Gospel to people that went to the County and State
Fairs in my mission. (At least that's how it felt at times.) There are
several reasons that this is difficult. First of all, in the "Bible belt"
region there are all kinds of hecklers and preachers who would love to
spar with the missionaries about religion as long as there was a crowd.
Secondly, most people are not in a very religious mood who go to a fair.*

*I remember one time working the Arkansas State Fair in Little
Rock County. We had a heckler who kept asking us questions like: how*

many wives did we have, where are our horns, and things such as that. After having done these fairs for a while, it really got tiring to have to put up with people like that. I was about ready to give up that day. I guess you could say that I was down in the dumps. I dreamed of being in a "normal assignment" where I could actually teach and commit people instead of just introducing the gospel all day and collecting referrals for the Elders in the Area. As I was talking to a group of fair-goers, I stopped for a second and said a silent prayer for help. Then feeling that I had better keep going for a while more, I proceeded to explain the message of the Restoration to this group.

I didn't know what to expect that day in that stuffy little circus tent we had, but I sure wished the Lord would call down some lightning on that heckler. All of a sudden the entire crowd went quiet. There was a hush that fell upon the crowd, because there was a motorcycle gang that had just pulled up. This motorcycle gang used to terrorize the Little Rock area. They were called the Road Warriors. They were visiting the fair and decided to wander past the Mormon tent. I remember the heckler turning to the head of that gang, a stout fellow of about 285 pounds, no shirt on, more hair than a gorilla, wearing a levi jacket with the arms cut out and on the back it said, "We're coming for your daughters-The Little Rock Road Warriors." The heckler figured that he could enlist the help of them in badgering the Mormon Elders.

When he turned to him, the head of the gang picked him up and said, "You got something wrong with these Mormons?"

The heckler turned red as a beet. The motorcyclist tore into him and told him to leave us alone. When the heckler started to complain about this rough treatment, the motorcycle gang leader threw him out of the tent, like I'd toss a pop can into the trash. The crowd cheered over the heckler's dismissal, and I proceeded to bear my testimony of the restored gospel to this group of people and the motorcycle gang.

When we were through, I went up to the gang leader and asked him why he helped us out. He said, "We know a Mormon who has always been nice to us and never cheated us." He said that he considered us to be his brothers. To this day I will never forget that experience of how the Lord answered my prayers and came to my rescue. Never again will I judge someone by their clothes or appearance. The Lord truly is the father of us all, even a motorcycle gang member at the Little Rock Arkansas County Fair.

• • •

The day of your missionary farewell you can't imagine your mission being anything but triumphant . . . but try tracting in freezing weather for two weeks; having a cold for a month, and trying to encourage a homesick companion, and wondering how you are going to eat for the next three weeks on twelve dollars. Triumph?! Heck, all you want to do is survive. But a mission should not be just a survival mission. You shouldn't just endure problems when you can overcome them.

So when things are really bleak, try these suggestions.

One, read inspirational material. It may come from a Church magazine, the scriptures, the autobiography of Parley P. Pratt, or your own journal. One of my favorite stories is by Oscar Kirkham about an old lamplighter in France.

I stood one day in far-off France with a group of boys about me. The colorful old lamplighter came with his interesting cape and his stiff-brimmed hat. He started to light the lamps. He lit this one; then he crossed the way and lit another. Then again, and this one did not burn very easily; he had to go up the post and clean it out. He was patient, and finally the light came on. We smiled, and he crossed the way again. By and by down the highway he went, and over into the city, and came again on the distant hilltop. We watched with interest to see this great pathway of light-one man lighting the highway. And so it may be with us in our missionary service. It may be difficult here or there. The light may not come on very easily, but with patience, with constant striving, and with prayer in our hearts, the highway will be made light, a safe place to travel.

I can't help thinking about that story when I am faced with something that is difficult or that I can't personally see a lot of progress on. Your missionary work will have a profound influence on other people's lives if you center your thoughts away from your own difficulties and onto the Cross of Christ.

Two, look for ways to overcome problems. Try dressing warmer and eating healthier to overcome that persistent cold. Convince your homesick companion that your mission area is really much nicer than back home. Make a pledge not to mention anything negative, or the one that makes a negative comment has to buy the other an ice cream cone or treat of their choice.

Three, be of good cheer. Missionaries who can remain cheerful despite their daily trials realize that whatever their challenges, life is still good. It still offers positive rewards each day. N. Eldon Tanner had some very good words to say on this matter.

> *Have a good time. That was the slogan we had in the West European Mission: Have a good time. I would like you all to have a good time."*
>
> *I said this to a group of missionaries in Germany one day. After the meeting, one of the missionaries came up to me and he said, "President Tanner, I don't think that it is quite fair for you to tell the missionaries to have a good time. You know, the only way they can have a good time is to do their work."*
>
> *I said, "Well, go have a good time."*

Four, accept criticism. A man moved into a small farming community and was soon made bishop. He was humbled by the calling and felt the responsibility that came with it. Accordingly, he would frequently get up before the congregation and give lengthy sermons on various aspects of the gospel that he felt his ward needed help with. Many times he would take an entire meeting preaching on one subject. But in spite of his efforts at "feeding his flock," he was dismayed to see many ward members yawning or falling asleep during his sermons. As he walked along a dirt road one day, thinking about this problem, he came upon a dairyman, a member of his ward, who was walking in the same direction. Feeling like he needed to talk to someone about his worries, he stated the problem to the man and asked him what he thought of it.

"Well, bishop," the dairyman said, "you've been good for us since you've been made bishop, and we appreciate it. We're obliged for your intentions and know that what you tell us is good, but you preach too long! Speaking for myself, I'm a lot like my milk cans. You can put only so much in one of those cans and then it will hold no more. And once it's filled to the brim, if you try to put any more in, even if it's the best milk in the world, it will only be spilled on the ground and wasted."

Now, that Bishop could have reacted one of two ways. Either he could have gotten insulted, blown his stack, yelled and screamed at this member and left in a huff, or he could have accepted what was given in the manner in which it was given, as merely a suggestion of an area that could be improved. It was given in love. Your mission President may not approve of all your ideas, a mission leader may chastise or correct you in an area that you feel they are totally in the wrong. Or they may be totally right and you are too proud to admit your error. In any case, please. Accept criticism. Thank the giver. If they are totally wrong, it's not worth arguing about.

Five, quality baptisms are more important than quantity. Elder Orsen F. Whitney's comments on this subject are extremely valid.

While on my first mission in the Eastern States I was asked:

"Why don't you 'Mormon' elders fly for higher game? Why do you always preach to the poor and lowly? Why don't you get up among the high and mighty? Take Henry Ward Beecher, for instance. Convert him, and his whole congregation would flock in after him; and just see how that would build up your Church."

"That is not God's way of building up His Church," I replied. "The Lord declared by an ancient prophet, 'I will take you one of a city, and two of a family, and I will bring you to Zion: and I will give you pastors according to mine heart.'" (Jeremiah 3:14-15)

I explained the great problem of the dispersions and gathering of Israel, whereby the blood of Abraham, Isaac, and Jacob, the blood that believes, with spirits answering to that blood, who have been dispersed for a wise purpose among all nations, are now being recalled and brought together in a great movement called "The Gathering," preparatory to the building of the New Jerusalem and the glorious coming of the Lord.

And I added, "God is not anxious for great congregations. He is not desirous that any one person or people should make a bargain with Him and join His Church as a business proposition."

I cannot describe in words my own personal conflict as I heard friends of mine describe "hitting over a hundred baptisms" when I was working 80 hours a week and being glad to have 5 first discussions a week and to have loaned out a dozen Books of Mormon. Don't accept the fact that your mission has a low baptismal record, but instead accept the fact that you are tool in your Heavenly Fathers hand. You can't arm-twist people into the Gospel. You wouldn't ever want someone to do that. Instead do your best. If the only soul which you bring unto Christ is "your own", then your joy shall be great because you tried your best.

Six, missions aren't always easy. I love reading stories like this one of Wilford Woodruff's from the Journal of Discourses.

In my early missions, when preaching in the Southern States — Arkansas, Tennessee, and Kentucky —I have waded swamps and rivers and have walked seventy miles or more without eating. In those days we counted it a blessing to go into a place where there was a Latter-day Saint. I went once 150 miles to see one, and when I got there he had apostatized, and tried to kill me. Then, after travelling seventy-two miles without food, I sat down to eat my meal with a Missouri mobocrat, and he damning and cursing me all the time . . . In those days we might travel hundreds and hundreds of miles and you could not find a Latter-day Saint, but now, thank God, we have the privilege of travelling hundreds and hundreds of miles where we can find but little else. I regard this as a great blessing.

When you feel discouraged and want to give up, remember that Brigham Young carried a Book of Mormon around in his pocket for an entire year before the missionary who converted him came and bore his testimony that he knew it to be true. Seek for the honest in heart and bear your testimony to them. Give as many people the opportunity to hear the gospel message as you can; be aware that many times you will be planting the seed that will bear fruit long into the future.

I could carry on for pages with positive statements about good attitudes, PMA, motivation, etc. But I honestly believe that after all has been said and done that is just whipped cream on your hot fudge sundae. The most important ingredient to keeping going is your own personal testimony and commitment to Christ.

Before you enter the mission field, commit yourself to serving the allotted time with cheerfulness, with determination to work diligently to share the gospel with everyone you can possibly reach, and with heartfelt commitment to Christ and His teachings. Do everything you can to bring love of Christ and of your fellowman to the mission field with you.

Challenge

Talk with a returned missionary you know about what they did to get them out of the rut when they got depressed or down on their missions.
